# The Gift of Mediumship

**Also from Mastery Press:**

*A Legacy of Love*
*Volume One: The Return to Mount Shasta and Beyond*

*To Master Self is to Master Life*

*Awaken the Sleeping Giant*

*A Wanderer in the Spirit Lands*

# The Gift of Mediumship

## Crossing the Bridge Between Two Worlds with a Lifelong Medium and His Master Guide

PHILIP BURLEY

Phoenix, Arizona

**Mastery Press**
P.O. Box 43548
Phoenix, AZ 85080
MasteryPress@gmail.com

First Edition

ISBN: 978-1-883389-14-7

Printed in the United States of America

**Philip Burley and Saint Germain portraits**
**by Elinor Mavor, Scottsdale, Arizona**

Cover and interior design
by 1106 Design, Phoenix, Arizona

# Dedication

*I gratefully dedicate this book to my heavenly Father, to my dear earthly spiritual teachers, to those in spirit who lovingly and tirelessly helped me to become a bridge between the physical and spiritual worlds, and to the wonderful people I have had the privilege of serving with my spiritual abilities.*

# Acknowledgments

MY THANKS GO TO EVERYONE who helped to bring this book into existence, including the helpful and responsive staff at 1106 Design in Phoenix, Arizona, Michele DeFilippo and Ronda Rawlins, and at Cadence Group in Watervliet, New York, Amy Collins MacGregor and Bethany Brown. They all helped with the important finishing touches.

Elinor Mavor's beautiful artwork has added much to this book. I am also grateful to Udo Brossmann, Lynn Mathers, David Flores, and my wife Vivien for their thorough reading and thoughtful commentary. Anne Edwards worked closely with me to bring real-life experiences into language and perspective that best convey them to the reader. I appreciate her excellent editing skills.

I am deeply grateful to my dear friend, Marie Wilson, for her ongoing support and loving devotion to this work. I also appreciate the wonderful people who asked lively and insightful questions in public presentations and in readings given across the nation and in Japan. Saint Germain's personal responses to all of them are an integral part of this book.

This book would be greatly diminished without the lives and work of gifted mediums Joan Donnelly Brooks, Chrisley

Witt, and Reed Brown, who taught me much by example and brought my spiritual guides through with such evidential messages. My eternal gratitude goes to those loving beings in the spirit world who appear throughout the pages of this book. In many ways, this is their story.

# Contents

# Preface

It gives me great happiness to share part of my story, including how the grace of heaven helped me to become a professional medium and channel for the spiritual master Saint Germain. *Part I* of this book describes how my work has evolved over more than two decades, and I hope it will take away the mystery surrounding mediumship. It includes answers I have given to questions over the years, excerpts from spiritual readings I have received, and some information from my personal records and previous publications. *Part II* provides insight into Saint Germain's teaching based on edited transcripts of several question-and-answer sessions in which he spoke through me. It represents a substantial example of the results of my work as a medium and channel.

I received the gifts of spiritual sight and hearing at an early age, and I have continued to have mystical experiences during most of my life. However, it was not until my mid-forties that a series of experiences led me to a formal study of mediumship and the beginning of my full-time practice in the mid-1980s. Since then, I have been encouraged in this work by affirming spiritual readings and the constant presence of my guides, Kathryn Kuhlman, Dr. Daniel David Palmer, Black Hawk, and Saint Germain. I have also been deeply touched and motivated by clients who report that readings have blessed them with healing and a deeper relationship with their own spiritual teachers and with God.

Of central importance to my work is my association with Saint Germain, a spiritual master and true representative of God—a friend and guide who has channeled God's wisdom and love directly through me for more than twenty-one years. His words, thoughts, and energy resonate with mine because of our close association, but they transcend anything I could offer alone. I am among many who receive healing when Saint Germain speaks, because he comes from the highest realms of spirit. He seeks no disciples but encourages each person to find God as a first step to finding peace and freedom in our human world.

Early on a day when Saint Germain is going to channel through me, I sometimes feel him nearby and experience adjustments that are already occurring within my spirit and body. When the audience assembles and Saint Germain is ready to speak, I usually have to clear my throat in a pronounced way because he is already in my aura or energy field. When this happens, I consciously step out of the way, so that he can speak directly through my vocal cords. People with the gift of clairvoyance say that they see my spirit come out of my body and step to one side, and they see Saint Germain, surrounded by gold and purple light, come into my body. Seeing his energy, they have attested to the magnitude of his presence.

Anyone who channels spirit will tell you that it takes a significant expenditure of energy to allow one's body to be used in this way. It requires discipline to stay spiritually focused and prepared so that spirit can come through clearly. In spite of this, I am grateful and honored that Saint Germain, a spiritual master of tremendous love and wisdom, has chosen to speak directly through me to thousands of people. His consistent message is that we can meet the loving presence of God whenever we turn inward, and he speaks more deeply and directly about God and human experience as the years go by.

Saint Germain works so closely with the master Jesus that I experience them as twin flames. The hallmark of each of their personalities is divine, unconditional love. Especially in individual readings, Saint Germain touches people at a very deep level, and many cry in his presence. He doesn't purposely provoke tears, but he comes so gently and works so kindly with individuals that he moves their hearts.

Today, many mediums channel spiritual masters or receive messages, and various teachers are bringing spiritual truth into the world. More and more people understand the existence of universal consciousness and our essential connection to God and to each other. This growing awareness is cutting across religious lines to lift humanity, helping to usher in a new spiritual age. Confusion may arise because of differences in the details of various teachings and modern revelations. Is there a spiritual roadmap to follow in these times? I believe there is.

Saint Germain teaches that we can find our direction by looking within. Rather than affirming specific beliefs or predictions about the future, he suggests that we develop our spiritual awareness to the point that we can discern what truth to embrace and what steps to take next. He encourages us to be increasingly attentive to our inner voice, and he guides us, above all else, to find true love with God and each other. We all long for limitless love that we can trust. In every book we read, in every quiet moment, we can listen for the voice that belongs to one who knows us completely and loves us absolutely. We can listen for God's voice within.

After many years of working as a professional medium and channel, I still find that the most important feature of my work and of my life is my relationship with God. I do not experience God as an anthropomorphic figure on a throne but as an infinite energy of exquisite personal love. I am aware of this love whenever I move into a meditative state or simply turn my attention inward. I feel an almost immediate transition into an altered state, sometimes called the alpha state, and I am flooded with a presence I recognize as God. To the degree that I remain aware of God's love and practice humility, I am confident that my work will progress in a direction that benefits many.

This is not a how-to book, but if you want to open your spiritual senses, learning about my experience may help you take another step in that direction. Whether or not you feel this calling, my greatest wish is that you will better understand authentic mediumship and channeling, and that you will realize the great importance of your own spiritual search. My prayer is that you will have a greater awareness of the loving beings from the highest realms who are with you at all times, supporting and guiding you throughout your life. They want only to help you find God.

Many have reported that the spiritual readings I have given have been life-changing for them. I take no credit for this, except for lending my energies to divine spiritual beings who have healed, loved, and touched through me. No medium has the solution to another's life, and I invite you to look within yourself for God and for your own truth. Ultimately, you have the answers to all of your questions. You have the inner resources to deal with whatever life brings. You have the ongoing support of loved ones who have died and the constant care of teachers and guides in spirit. Most of all, you have God.

My thanks go to all who read this book for allowing me the opportunity to share with you some of my life as a human being and as a bridge between this world and the next. I thank those working with me in spirit and God who sent them for the great gift of mediumship. My life has been a walk made possible by divine grace. Please read the following pages with your own good judgment at hand and with a heart that is open to words that may take root in your soul and guide you to that place within where we all meet—in the loving embrace of God.

— Philip Burley

# Part I

# Opening the Door Within

*Questions and Answers with Philip Burley*

# Early Experiences and Training

***Q: How did you become a medium?***

PB: I began having spiritual experiences when I was a child, and I can't remember a time when I did not know God. From the time I was four years old, I prayed night after night for my family, the world, and anything else that I knew about. I really couldn't fall asleep until I prayed.

When I was a very small child, even younger than four, spirits began to visit me at my bedside. I often told my mother about these visitors, and she would tell others. She said this happened many times while I was growing up. I remember that the first to come was St. Anthony, who materialized and spoke to me again years later in a room full of people who all saw and heard him.

My St. Anthony is an unknown fifteenth-century German monk—a different individual from St. Anthony of Padua, who lived in the thirteenth century.

I have continued to have spiritual experiences as an adult: Many years ago, an angel visited me in a dream and said that he was sent by the Father to tell me that my mission was to help Christians gain a greater understanding of the spirit world and spiritual life. Later, when I was doing radio shows as a medium, Jesus often came to guide me regarding what to share with listeners. Saint Germain, Jesus, Mother Mary, and various spirits still wake me up, with a message for me or someone else.

Though all people are mediumistic to some degree, I was born with an ability that developed at an early age through my relationship with God, my prayer life, and the attendance and guidance of the spirit world. At the age of forty-six, while involved in secular work, I finally realized that I had to follow the direction of my spiritual awareness and gifts. I knew I had to seek proper training to develop my gifts as a medium. That is what I did, and I have never looked back. This conscious decision was my first step toward becoming a full-time professional medium.

***Q: Can you talk more about your experience of knowing God at such an early age?***

PB: I was born at home in a small town called Waynedale, a suburb of Fort Wayne, Indiana. When I was four years old, our family moved to a farm with seventy-five acres of land about fifteen miles southwest of my birthplace. Our house was one hundred years old and made with hand-hewn pine beams held together with wooden pegs. All the nails used in the construction were handmade—the old-fashioned square type. The walls were covered with plaster containing horsehair to strengthen it and hold it together. There was no electricity in the house, so our lighting came from kerosene lamps. We had no indoor plumbing, and our outhouse was located a long way from the back door.

Today I realize that God moved me to that farm so that I would wander through the fields and woods where I had my most significant spiritual experiences. I was in a state of awe and ecstasy as I walked in nature, experiencing the personal and tender presence of God. I would converse with God just as I am talking with you now, and I heard God speaking to me in a most tangible way. Through these experiences, I came to realize even more fully how real God is and how much he loves each one of us. I can understand St. Francis very well, as he was also caught up in praising and adoring God when he was alone in nature, in prayer.

***Q: You have described having out-of-body experiences since early childhood. Can you explain what that was like?***

PB: I was always eager to go to bed at night, because as soon as I lay down, I would go under very rapidly and find my spirit rising up from my body. Most people don't realize it, but all of us have out-of-body experiences. Have you felt a jerking sensation that wakes you up just as you're falling asleep? When I ask audiences how many have felt this, most people put their hands up, because it's a universal experience.

You feel this sensation when your spirit body rises up out of your physical body and then suddenly returns. When finally free from the earthly vibration, your spirit may rise and hover five or six feet above your body or travel into the spirit world to visit deceased loved ones, attend a spiritual class, meet with your guides and teachers, or just receive spiritual renewal. Whether you are hovering near your sleeping body or traveling away from it, you are unconsciously taking in vitally needed *spiritual energy* before returning to your body.

As a child, I was wide awake and aware when this was happening to me. As my spirit rose from my body, I could see the bed and everything else in my room. At the side of the bed, I could see a solid gold rock, about the size of a football, which glowed from within with a light that was so bright that it lit up the room until there were no shadows anywhere. When I looked up, I could see the ceiling getting closer and closer, and when I looked down and to my right, I could see the rock. The higher I rose, the larger the rock became, until it was the size of a large boulder, taking up half the room. As it grew, it continued to shine brilliantly with a golden light from within. Of course, I thought all people rose up out of their bodies at night to see brilliantly glowing, expanding rocks by their beds!

After observing the rock, while still in spirit and out of my body, I often continued to rise through the ceiling and into the spirit world, where I studied with the masters in preparation for my life's work.

Many years later, spirit came to me and said that the rock in my room represented God and Christ. I was told that just as the rock grew gradually in my room, God would increasingly fill my life as I grew older and moved further on my path. Now I see that my experience with the rock was really a prophecy, and I am very touched by all that spirit did for me.

*Q: You talk about receiving classical mediumship instruction. What is classical mediumship?*

PB: Some people go into mediumship after reading a book about it, attending classes or having experiences in personal meditations. Others are natural mediums who start practicing without any kind of training. Classical mediumship involves learning systematically how to open the spiritual senses. Students sit in a circle with an experienced medium and are actually able to borrow from the mediumistic energy of their teacher. The teacher's guides come from the spirit world to help instruct the students.

I had a very fine teacher, Joan Donnelly Brooks, who led by example rather than giving detailed instruction. Under her auspices and in her presence, I gained much of my skill as a medium. In that setting the spiritual environment was so prepared that there was a strong probability that my spiritual senses would open if I had genuine mediumistic abilities. Divine teachers from the spirit world guided me to understand my own clairvoyance and clairaudience. For three years, I traveled one hundred miles round trip every Saturday to sit with my teacher for two hours of training. My wife Vivien and I both studied in this way.

The transference of energy from the medium to the student was an important part of the training I received from

Joan. I once heard English medium Doris Collins speak of this transference, and I saw her clearly demonstrate it. Collins was well known throughout England for her healing work, and since Vivien and I were traveling in England, we decided to go to a town northeast of London to hear her speak. While we were there, she asked a young man who had never done anything like this before if he would come up and try out his mediumistic skill. She put her right hand on his back, and he opened up completely, suddenly able to see clairvoyantly. In fact, he gave me an absolutely accurate reading. As soon as the medium took her hand off his back, he could no longer see clairvoyantly.

Collins demonstrated that she could transmit energy to initiate people into spiritual openness. This particular ability is part of the picture of classical mediumship.

***Q: As you were studying mediumship, spirits visibly manifested themselves to you. Can you describe how this actually happens?***

PB: Classical mediumship can include phenomena where spiritual beings, animals, and objects materialize in the room through the medium's particular talents. That happened in the environment where I received my training, though few mediums demonstrate this ability today.

The reason that we generally cannot see spirits is that they exist in a dimension that vibrates at a higher frequency than can be seen or felt using our physical senses. To achieve visible materializations, spirits use ectoplasm, a moldable energy that comes from the medium. When working this way, some mediums use a red light in the room, because its wavelength doesn't affect ectoplasm, while white light causes it to break down. Materializations take shape at varying levels of density according to the amount of ectoplasm the medium is able to provide and the degree to which spirits lower their own vibrational frequency to become visible to our physical senses. A spiritual being may appear fleetingly or for a longer time. The appearance may be so ethereal that your hand can pass through the vision as though passing through air, or so solid that you can touch the spiritual form and feel a physical reality.

Depending on the particular gifts of the medium, another way that spirits manifest themselves is by making their voices audible through their use of trumpets. Shaped like a megaphone and made of lightweight metal, trumpets used for this purpose are about seven inches in diameter on the larger end and about a half-inch in diameter on the smaller end, and they can be collapsed to make them easy to carry. Spirits use energy from the medium (ectoplasm) to literally build a spirit voice box or larynx inside the trumpet, which they then use to make and magnify sound. When trumpets are used, the spirit speaking is not usually seen.

I have been present with others when up to four trumpets were floating in the air with no apparent support. I could actually see two lines of energy, or ectoplasm, which looked like white gossamer threads emanating from the physical vocal cords of the medium and running through the small end of a trumpet to connect to the spiritual voice box inside. While the medium was in a trance state, spirits used his energy as a battery or transformer to lower their own energy so that it could pass into and through him. They could then send their energy down the two gossamer lines and speak aloud through one of the floating trumpets.

***Q: What were some of your actual experiences with spirit manifestations?***

PB: On one occasion, Vivien and I saw a little guide materialize in the middle of the room about five feet from where we were sitting. First, a pool of light appeared as though a spotlight were shining in the room. Rising from that light, as the energy moved, we could see the bottom of the hem of a long skirt. More of the skirt started to take form, and then the torso of a little girl appeared. Finally her arms, neck, and head took shape until there she stood, totally materialized in front of us. Her voice could be clearly heard when she asked, "Do you want to see the power of spirit?" No one said no! She said, "Okay, I'll change from being a little girl to being an old woman." Just like that, she shifted her shape into that of a little old woman, still standing in front of us. It was almost unbelievable but at the same time beautiful to see this manifestation of the power of spirit.

Another time, a gypsy named Madam Clara materialized in the room accompanied by a black leopard. Clara said, "Don't be afraid, because in the spirit world, animals are not dangerous. They don't fight, and they won't bite you." As the leopard walked around, bumping against our legs, we could hear him purr. In the darkness, I reached out, felt his fur, the warmth of his body, and the vibration that rippled through his torso when he growled. At one point, he jumped up and put his front paws on the knees of a woman who laughed and screamed at the same time. It was a most amazing experience and a clear demonstration of the literal presence and power of spirit.

One of the most interesting experiences occurred when a spiritual guide named Morning Star stood fully materialized in front of us and asked, "Would you like to hear my life story?" She told us that she was a Native American who had been in the spirit world for six hundred years. She said she had been kidnapped by a hostile tribe, taken as a captive to their compound, and put into a pit full of poisonous snakes, which is how she died. The memory of this experience was still so vivid that Morning Star began to cry as she told her story. Though she was present in the beginning to guide us through that evening, she couldn't continue with us and had to go back into the spirit world. Another spirit guide came to lead the session.

One night about fifteen of us were gathered with a trumpet medium when St. Paul appeared and spoke to us in an audible voice through the trumpet floating in the air. The whole room was filled with the fragrance of roses as he spoke, and the atmosphere was one of great peace, moving everyone to reverent silence. This amazing experience is recorded on a tape in my archives.

***Q: Did any of the spirits who materialized in such a tangible way bring a personal message for you?***

PB: Kathryn Kuhlman, the famous spiritual healer, was one of the first to make herself known to me using the trumpet, though the medium had no idea that she would appear. She talked directly to me about my future as a healer and leader and said that I would see her hands over mine when I did healing work. This has happened. Over time, a number of my guides and teachers spoke through the trumpet, and all of these messages were recorded and transcribed. Each message was an important milestone for me as I worked to establish a foundation for my work, and they offer fresh guidance and inspiration each time I refer to them.

One special night, I was surprised when Morning Star said, "Uncle Philip, I have someone here for you who calls himself 'Brother.'" I immediately knew that it was St. Anthony, the first guide to appear to me when I was a child. Only Vivien and I knew that he had any role in my life, and only I knew that I had always addressed him as "Brother Anthony." St. Anthony emerged from a curtained cabinet in which the medium was sitting. Dressed all in white, he looked as though he were made of light, and he called me to come up. As I stood in front of him, I could clearly see that he was a spiritual being because of his luminous face and the light emanating from his attire. We were so close that I could see the threads in the fabric of his hooded robe. He prayed and spoke to the rest of those gathered about having worked with me. The room was filled with a powerful energy of love, and there was such sacredness in this experience that many of us were softly crying.

At the time of this extraordinary encounter, I was in my mid-forties, and it was so moving to have St. Anthony appear in this way and validate the bedside experience of a small boy. There is no question in my mind that I am not the exception.

All people have spirit guides and teachers who have worked with them from birth.

These are only some of the outstanding spirit manifestations that I could tell you about. They were the result of the unique spiritual gifts of mediums that I visited while I was learning more about my own mediumship. Some of what I saw, heard, and felt is hard to convey in words, and I only wish that more people could have been with me to share these increasingly rare experiences.

***Q: You are able to recall verbatim statements made long ago by various spirits because they were recorded. Have you documented all of your spiritual encounters?***

PB: From the time I began my formal training in mediumship until today, I have recorded and preserved all of the readings I have given or received, as well as my private spiritual experiences. After more than twenty-one years, I have volumes of recordings and written material, and I am working to transcribe, organize, and store all of this material so that it can be useful to me and to others in the future. I am grateful to the wonderful people who are helping with this tremendous undertaking.

One reason for documenting my experience is that I want a record of the guidance I receive from spirit for my own use. Another reason is that the guidance that comes through for me or for others often has universal applications for anyone seeking spiritual growth. I have written books based on information that I have received from spirit, through readings from other mediums, private journaling, or spiritual channeling.

I have recorded dreams, prayer experiences, and every communication that has had significant bearing on my decisions and the direction of my work over the course of time.

One example of the importance of documentation and record keeping is the compelling request I received in a private meditation almost three years ago. Spirit urgently asked me to encourage as many people as possible to pray for America and the world. The request was validated by subsequent profound prayer experiences, but also by a vivid spiritual dream that I'd had several years earlier. Though I could not know it at the time, the dream was prophetic of September 11, 2001. Its message was to become the foundation of the prayer project that I was guided to coordinate beginning in 2005 and continuing today. I might not have realized the significance of the request for prayer if I had not kept a detailed account of my earlier dream. As it was, I was able to share my experiences accurately with all of the people on my mailing list, and many joined in the prayer effort because of this. I never know what will be of critical importance, so I document everything.

Another reason I record spiritual readings is so that people can listen to their readings more than once or transcribe them for ongoing reference. I hear that this helps people to internalize the guidance they receive, and they sometimes gain meaningful new insights when they review the material. The same thing is true for me.

Frequently the spiritual messages that come through are at such a level that they have significance beyond the time when they are given. They are not intended only to provide a fleeting moment of inspiration, healing, or blessing, but to provide ongoing guidance to me and to others for our walk in this world.

***Q: Even though you have been spiritually open since childhood, you did not become a professional medium until you were in your mid-forties. Why do you think it happened then?***

PB: Though it can happen earlier in life, many mediums begin their work in their middle years because it can take much preparation and experience to know beyond a doubt that you are literally seeing, hearing, and feeling spirit. Emmanuel Swedenborg, a versatile man and talented inventor, was fifty-six years old when he fully experienced his mediumistic abilities and wrote about them.

Before I became a medium, I was working as the project manager for a company that was building office space in the Washington, D.C., area. A few employees who were also close friends knew about my spiritual experiences and said, "Philip, you know you're in the wrong field." Having been spiritually aware all my life, I realized that my nature and experience were still pointing in the direction of living a life centered on spiritual work, and I continued to think about this possibility.

While I was still working in Washington, Vivien and I went to the Arlington Metaphysical Chapel in Arlington, Virginia, where the minister Reed Brown was doing readings for people in the congregation. When he turned to me he said, "I don't know who you are, but you're an old soul, and you have to be involved in spiritual work! You're a natural healer. I see blue light pouring out of your hands and out of your solar plexus. The American flag is wrapped completely around you, and you were born for this country. Your mission is for this country." He said more, but that was the gist of his message. He also did a meaningful reading for Vivien, encouraging her in her own spiritual journey.

As we walked across the parking lot that night, I turned to Vivien with tears in my eyes and asked, "Why does it take so long to know exactly who you are and what you are supposed to do in life?" She just smiled and looked at me. Not long after that evening, I learned about Joan Donnelly and trumpet mediumship. Though Joan's classes were at least fifty miles from our home, Vivien and I visited Joan right away, and she accepted us as students.

***Q: When did you first begin to give readings to people?***

PB: Joan was the head of an organization called Silver Belle, which had chapel facilities in Ephrata, Pennsylvania. Vivien and I not only sat with Joan in training but also attended services at the chapel, where she asked her students to give spiritual messages to those gathered. From the beginning, it felt natural to me to give readings, but it takes great patience and time to go through the attunement process to the point where you can accurately see and hear the spirit world. Like any skill, you have to practice through trial and error until you get it right.

We were approximately a year and a half into our training when Joan asked me to give some spiritual messages to the congregation. While still learning, I did my best, and I was satisfied with my offerings to individuals in that setting. In fact, I felt greatly encouraged about my decision to become a professional medium. My teacher told me periodically that I was a finely attuned instrument, and the readings I gave in training were accurate enough to keep me motivated.

After almost two years of study and practice, I scheduled my first independent readings in the Washington, D.C. area. Without realizing the tremendous amount of energy required, I enthusiastically made fifteen appointments for forty-five-minute readings in one weekend! I was exhausted by Sunday night, but my spiritual work grew rapidly after that.

# Close Encounters: Saint Germain and Others

***Q: You have said you are a channel for Saint Germain. How did Saint Germain and your other spiritual guides first make themselves known to you?***

PB: I must begin with Kathryn Kuhlman's initial contact with me. One evening, I was in an almost empty library in Annandale, Virginia, near Washington, D.C., looking for an autobiography to read. As I walked through the stacks, a book moved out from the shelf toward me. I thought someone must have pushed it from the next aisle, but when I looked, no one was there. I picked up the book, *Daughter of Destiny,* and found that it was a biography of deceased healer Kathryn Kuhlman. That same weekend, Vivien and I were present at a small gathering where Kathryn Kuhlman spoke to me through the trumpet and materialized in the room. She was the first spirit guide to let me know that she was working with me specifically to help me develop my mediumship. Words cannot express the impact of such experiences on my heart and soul. They were pivotal in inspiring me to stay on the path toward becoming a medium.

***Q: How did you first encounter Saint Germain?***

PB: In August of 1986, I read a book by Guy Ballard about his *I AM* work, which is centered on Saint Germain. I felt as though I had come home, though I was not looking to find a leader or to join a group. Three weeks later, on Labor Day, 1986, I rose early to pray and meditate, after which I went back to sleep. About an hour later, I was awakened by a powerful and loving parental presence, and I knew I had entered another dimension. I was surrounded by an unearthly golden light, and I saw a golden path in front of me. The calm voice of my heavenly Father assured me that the path symbolized the course I was called to follow to fulfill my purpose on earth.

Still suspended in the embrace of heaven, I became aware of a different presence on the left side of the bed and immediately recognized it as that of the man I had read about in Ballard's book. I saw him clairvoyantly, gradually more clearly, and he was wearing a violet robe. He said, "Philip, this is Saint Germain. Rise and write, for I have something I want to say to you that I will pass on in your writings."

I hesitated because I didn't want to become dominated or controlled by the spirit world in some erroneous way. Saint Germain appeared to understand my reluctance and stood waiting patiently for me to think things through. Then he said, "Don't you realize that the spirit of all great spirits is one of cooperation?" I felt his sincerity and honesty, and I was moved by his obvious love, patience, and wisdom. In addition, who could doubt the brilliance of the light that surrounded him? I realized that great souls do rise above creed and nationality to demonstrate universality, and that for the sake of the whole they do seek cooperation. I got up and went to the dining room table with my journal and pen in hand.

I waited in silence for Saint Germain to appear again, and he manifested to my left, standing in a shimmering ray of white light. He looked ethereal, yet he appeared in full bodily form. He seemed to stand in a ray of white light from above, but he was also surrounded by light that appeared to come directly from his auric field, and the larger area around him was also bathed in light. I said telepathically, "I am here, and I am ready." As Saint Germain began to speak, his words were clearly audible, and he spoke for about forty-five minutes. Here is part of what he said:

> *The light that you seek is all around you. You are not, I repeat, are not in darkness. You have but to open your "eyes" to see its blinding reality. You are doing that now.*
>
> *Philip, my dear brother, many things are unfolding for you and are in store. You will not believe them because you will not believe that these things could or would happen to you. Take heart, Philip, there is a plan unfolding at this time—due to God's timetable—that makes it*

*possible for you and others around you to leap across normal time spans and know and do things with a rapidity normally unheard of on earth.*

*You have a [spiritual] host around you at your beck and call. . . . We here are well aware of your heart, your longing. . . . You will see the unfolding of a marvelous plan before your eyes. Take it in stride as it happens. . . . Praise God and his hosts for the work done.*

*The Western world is overripe for tying together all that is known and for the final stage of understanding to bring man out of the dark spiritual ages. . . . Be patient, be patient, be patient. Remember always, you are never alone. . . . But remain ever serving and humble to the Source of life—that is the key. Let [God] work through you [and maintain] humility and obedience to his voice. An inner knowingness guarantees safety and success. . . .*

*We are one long chain of workers. Because of us, you are able to know, be, and do today. We, more than you, are [eager] to complete this work, for we have endeavored for eons of time to raise man back to his Father, his creator. It is all we know—this work and its accompanying longing make up the vibration of the fabric of our spiritual garments. In this way, we reflect his presence and his will. This is the meaning of the Great White Brotherhood [also called "Ascended Masters"].*

After this first receiving from Saint Germain was over, I continued to write in my journal with some follow-up thoughts:

> *I return to myself with gratitude to Saint Germain. . . . More of this will happen as time unfolds, but I don't want to create the circumstances for the making of self-fulfilling prophecies. . . . I am always guided by a will to order. There cannot be just spiritual experiences; there must also be logic and order to them as well. This I always seek. . . .*

***Q: Have you ever thought that you dreamed or imagined such experiences?***

PB: It has always been important and meaningful to me to receive validation of messages I receive for others or for myself. I often seek this through prayer or through mindful observation of my dreams, thoughts, emotions, and input from others and my surroundings. My first encounter with Saint Germain was validated in an extraordinary way.

In the early afternoon of the same day that I first saw and heard Saint Germain, the five of us, Vivien and I and our three teen-aged children, took the fifty-mile drive to Ephrata, Pennsylvania, to attend a message service given by mediums at the spiritualist camp, Silver Belle. When we arrived, all of the sixty to seventy seats were filled except for five chairs placed side by side in the center of the front row. It was as if they had been saved just for our family. We sat down a few moments before the service began.

Through the open door leading to the chapel stage, I could see the visiting medium from Ohio, Reverend Chrisley Witt (now deceased). Dressed in soft yellow white-trimmed vestments, he was waiting for the moment to come onto the stage. He and I had been introduced briefly at an earlier gathering, and a demonstration of his mediumship at that time had left me certain that he was a good medium. I had no way of knowing that I was about to experience a further demonstration that would leave me almost speechless.

Chrisley, as we came to call him, finally came out onto the platform and stood at the lectern to give messages from the spirit world. Stepping to his right, he scanned the audience seeking spiritual guidance as to whom he was to give a message. I don't remember how many messages he gave to others before he addressed me, looking very serious. He turned his face to one side, closed his eyes, slightly bowed his head and rested his chin on his hands. For those of us who had seen this kind of demonstration, it was obvious that he was listening intently to spirit. His initial remarks indicated that his message was for me, and my response confirmed that to him. A suspenseful silence fell over the gathering as Chrisley turned to me with his eyes still closed and said, "You had an experience this morning very early, didn't you?"

I thought to myself, "This can't be happening," but responded by saying, "Yes, I did."

Chrisley said, "Yes, you did. You awakened real early this morning. All of a sudden you woke up."

I hadn't awakened suddenly, but I had been suddenly moved from a state of deep sleep to a state of consciousness where the spirit world could get my attention. Without arguing the finer points of the experience, I said, "Yes, I did."

Chrisley opened his eyes and asked, for the benefit of the rest of the audience, "Now you didn't tell me this, did you?"

"No, I did not," I said.

Closing his eyes again, as if shutting out the world to concentrate on the voice of spirit, Chrisley said, "No, you didn't. But you woke up very early and . . . had to get out of the bed and do some writing."

"That's right," I said in amazement.

He asked again, "Is that correct?"

"That's correct," I said with a broad smile on my face. This was an exquisite demonstration of spirit communication at its best. People in the room began to whisper among themselves, and the atmosphere was charged. I felt like the witness in a courtroom scene from a movie, with the audience waiting breathlessly for the outcome of the trial.

Chrisley was not about to stop. He was on a roll and definitely attuned to the powers above. He opened his eyes wide and said, "That's right. And you jumped up and got a pencil and paper." (It was a pen, not a pencil—another minor point.) He settled back into mediumistic reverie, pausing again to listen to spirit, and then said, "Now, as you were writing, you sensed the presence of the person that was doing this."

"Yes."

"And yet, you doubted a little bit in your mind if that really was the person who wrote through you. Is that right?"

In truth, I had not doubted the person's identity but had doubted myself and the content relayed through my writing. Again, Chrisley was far too accurate for me to argue the point, so I said, "Yes."

By this time, Chrisley was fully into the emotion of the moment and said, very dramatically, "You'd better believe it! Well, the person who wrote through you was Saint Germain!"

"Oh, bless him!" I exclaimed in awe.

"And you knew that, didn't you?" Chrisley asked.

"Yes, I did!" was all I could say.

Chrisley concluded, "Don't you ever doubt it again!"

Voices in the audience rose, belief mingled with disbelief. I was so deeply moved and grateful that all I could say was "Oh! Thank you so much. Thank you so much." This sensational, evidential reading had confirmed beyond a doubt that Saint Germain had indeed visited me that morning and that he would be an ongoing part of my life.

I can recall every detail of this day because I had my tape recorder running, and it caught every word and audible nuance of the experience. What I observed is etched in my memory as well. I know now that this first personal encounter with Saint Germain was pivotal and life changing, and I believe that it was all planned and orchestrated by him and higher powers. These experiences established the authenticity of my work, so that I could have confidence in my mediumship and continue to cooperate by making myself available for heaven's use.

***Q: Can you tell us more about your early experiences with Saint Germain and other spiritual guides?***

PB: During my training with Joan Donnelly, the trumpet went up one autumn night in 1986 and Dr. Daniel David Palmer, founder of chiropractic, spoke. He said that he was working with me and that when the snow fell, they would impress me with an important message. Next, Saint Germain came and told me that he was continuing to work with me and that he knew everything I had been through, but said little more. I scratched my head, wondering what these messages were all about. Everything flowed from that night.

As recorded in the transcript of an event in July 1987, Saint Germain came through the trumpet again, this time speaking to me at length. He materialized solidly in the room, put his hands on me, and did a healing. As he spoke, he was so close to me that I was aware of his breathing. He was right there with me and with other spirit guides, moving around in the room. Here are some of the actual words exchanged between Saint Germain and me, taken from the transcript of this meeting:

*SG: This is Saint Germain. I come in the golden and purple light of all that is holy and all that is filled with love. It's so great indeed that we can be with someone who is as dedicated as you are.*

**PB:** Oh, thank you. Not enough.... How can I increase my understanding and my sense of your presence? Is that on your side or my side?

**SG:** *It is on both sides. We must meet each other half way.*

**PB:** I see.

**SG:** *My advice to you would be to strengthen love within yourself—unselfish love.*

**PB:** Unselfish love.

**SG:** *Regardless of whether you like an individual, whether you appreciate what they do or do not do, love them totally and completely.*

**PB:** Yes.

**SG:** *Do not look at their faults and mistakes, but look at them as you.*

**PB:** Yes.

**SG:** *And love without any desire for a return.*

**PB:** Okay, I'll work on it.

**SG:** *That kind of love will bring me so close to you, and will cement me so intimately into your aura, that there will be a continual and perpetual moving together at all times.*

I can give only a portion of all that he said and everything that happened that day. I have no words to describe the reality of this awesome encounter with the master. That experience gave me spiritual wings, and my mission took flight.

Many other spiritual encounters followed, and in early January 1988, as the snow fell around our home in Pennsylvania, Saint Germain asked me to receive dictation from him every Sunday morning after my customary prayer and meditation time. I sat faithfully each week for this purpose, and these intimate communications became the highlight of my week. Sometimes other high-realm spirit beings, including the renowned English medium William Stainton Moses and the biblical figure Saint Paul would come to impart relevant and beautiful words. Their messages are interspersed among Saint Germain's words in my first book, *To Master Self is to Master Life.*

***Q: How did Saint Germain first begin to speak directly through your vocal cords?***

PB: I had been giving readings for about two years when I noticed a significant change in my vocal cords. I wondered if I was having temporary throat problems, but the change didn't go away, and my voice kept getting deeper. I was told by Saint Germain to go see Reed Brown again at the Arlington Metaphysical Chapel. Reed had seen me only in the audience at the chapel and had no personal knowledge about me or my work. I arranged for a private reading, and Reed sat across from me at a little table. With his eyes closed, he began to give me names, including those of my guides Dr. Palmer and Tiffany. "Tiffany" was the name Kathryn Kuhlman used when she first appeared to me in the guise of a child guide. He also talked about the work I was doing as a medium and about my organization, Adventures in Mastery or AIM.

By this time, because of the powerful spiritual energies in the room, I already had my eyes closed and found myself, without controlling the process, going into a trance-like state, filled with unbelievable peace and detachment from anything earthly. I had never experienced such a thing in all of my life. Then I heard Reed rubbing his hands rapidly together and saying, "Ah! Saint Germain!"

I remained in trance as this masterful medium got up and came around the table to place his right hand about two inches from my lower abdomen. He then moved his hand vertically past my chest and face to the top of my head. As he did this, I felt a powerful energy, accompanied by intense heat, going up my whole torso, spine, throat, and head. Reed said, "Saint Germain wants to speak through you. Let him speak."

Saint Germain stepped in and spoke through my vocal cords. I could hear him saying to Reed, "We've been trying to get through to this young man to tell him that he has this gift and that we want to use him for this purpose. Thank you very much." Later I listened to the tape recording of this initiation into spirit channeling to be sure that I had heard it correctly.

From that time on, whenever I have done readings, Saint Germain has overshadowed me and spoken directly to people through me. I go into such a deep trance that I no longer hear what he says when he speaks through me. I catch some words, usually at the beginning or at the end of the channeling session, and I am clearly aware of his unique energy of love. Clairvoyant people watching me channel Saint Germain have said that they actually see me step out of and stand beside my body, and they see him moving in. Anyone who has heard me channel him knows that his voice has distinctive characteristics. He uses my vocal cords, and to some extent my vocabulary, but his voice is consistently at a lower register than my voice.

For more than two decades, Saint Germain has continued to speak through me to bring helpful and healing words to countless people through spiritual readings for individuals and groups.

# Being a Medium

***Q: Is there a difference between being a medium and being psychic?***

PB: In my experience, psychics work with mental energy, perceiving the reality of the spirit world primarily through their minds. Examples include what is often called extrasensory perception or mind-reading. Mediums actually see or hear the spirit world through spiritual senses such as clairvoyance or clairaudience, and this makes the information very real and present. An example would be the tangible appearance of a spirit being who may communicate through spoken words, images, or impressions. Words may be spoken without a vision, or a vision may appear without words. There are likely to be varying degrees of both gifts in one person, so there is no hard line between being psychic and being a medium. It's just that mediums have the specific ability to actually see and hear the spirit world.

***Q: People say you are as much mystic as medium. What does that mean to you?***

PB: Many people today are developing mediumistic abilities through reading how-to books or attending classes in spiritual development. They may have a natural or learned ability to open their spiritual senses, but to be grounded in true spirituality is to be grounded in the presence of God. I have communicated regularly with God from the time I was a child until today. God has been as much or more a part of my life as people have been. I have heard God as a still, small voice inside, sometimes as a voice that was not so still and small, and sometimes as a voice outside of me. People ask how I know that I'm hearing the voice of God and not that of a spirit. Through my lifelong experience, I have learned that spirit speaks or appears from one side or direction, but the voice of God comes in 360 degrees on all planes and from all directions. That's the difference.

I pursued God consistently, not out of belief or faith but as a living reality. It was through that experience that my spiritual senses opened. This may be only one path to becoming mediumistic, but my relationship with God has been centrally important. Without it, I don't know that I would have become a medium. Knowing God was and is the leading point in my life.

***Q: How have your family and friends responded to your being in this profession?***

PB: Responses have varied, but I have never been rejected by anyone because of my work. The only thing that I want to accomplish is to awaken as many people as possible to God within and to the reality of the spirit world. That's it. People are hungry to know themselves, to know God, and to know the eternal destiny that is written within them. This desire is created in them just as seeds are created in an apple. When you speak rationally and lovingly about these things, people are not turned off; they're turned on. I don't come from a place that is holier-than-thou or from on high. I speak as honestly and sincerely as I can, and I don't have an agenda that I'm trying to promote. I never pretend or pull punches, and I speak what I know to be true. I think these are some of the reasons that my work has been well received.

Do I live this way perfectly? Not at all. I'm just like every person who ever struggled; and everyone has. That's the name of the game, and it's what our education on earth is about. You fall down ten times to get up the eleventh time, or a thousand times to get up a thousand and one times. It's the falling down and getting up that really teaches us, not being "perfect." If the earth were just one smooth ball with no mountains, it would be very boring, without interest or personal challenge. If there were no rough spots or mountains to climb in our lives, we could not grow.

I am grateful for the struggles I have experienced in my life. Without them, my spirit wouldn't have been refined by my having to weather life's ups and downs. I might have become prideful; I don't know. I do know that falling down is good, so that we can learn how to get up and stay up.

***Q: Are your spiritual senses open at all times, so that you can see a person's aura, or read a person's spiritual situation at will?***

PB: No, though sometimes I am able to do this more or less accidentally. If I feel a certain warmth or affection, even toward someone I meet briefly and casually, I may instantly know something about the person. On one occasion, I was with the teller at our bank whom I know only through that contact. Though I usually don't mention my profession, I told her that I was a medium, and she said, "Oh, I believe in all that." I said, "Looking at you, I get the feeling that you are a creative person who either plays the piano or sings." The words just came out of me. She said, "Yes, I'm a singer, and I'm going to school to study voice. I'm working here to make a living."

I felt a spiritual, not personal, affection and closeness to a person, and in that moment, spirit came near. Because I am like a sponge, I picked up some information.

***Q: It is said that a medium can become physically and emotionally depleted because of the amount of energy it takes to do the work. Have you experienced this?***

PB: Yes. I manage it by taking time off. Some mediums actually die young because they don't realize how much physical energy they use to bring spirit through. Each of us is allotted just so much physical energy, and when it is depleted, sometimes by overuse, there is no more left. Some people die sooner than they might have if they had been more attentive to their physical needs, regardless of their chosen work.

If you are doing spiritual work, you draw upon your reservoir of energy more than the average person does, and you deplete it sooner. The way to replenish yourself is to rest and do nothing. Stop your spiritual activity for a while. One of the most famous healers in England said that every year he went on a two-week cruise and read Western novels to rest from his work. Kathryn Kuhlman, one of my guides, went to Brazil for two weeks each year and did nothing but rest. As much as I can, I try to recreate myself by consciously taking time off, sometimes for a substantial period of time.

***Q: Do you find that your diet is important when you are doing intense spiritual work?***

PB: One thing that has always been true about me is that I eat to live and don't live to eat. I like good food, but it's not of great importance, so it may be easier for me than it is for some to be careful about my diet. I seldom drink alcohol because I usually have to work the next day, and I know that I am susceptible to alcohol in the sense that it just puts me out. I like the taste, but not the effect, so I just stay away from it. I drink water frequently and try to eat a balanced diet including vegetables and fruit. I'm not as attracted to red meat as I used to be, though I still have it occasionally.

***Q: How do you maintain a sound direction in your personal life and in your work as a medium?***

PB: One of the most important things in my life is prayer. I do not pray out of obligation but because I meet God, and that connection has been there since childhood. If I veer from my habit of prayer, I feel lost; not like a child who has let go of his parent's hand, but like a person who has lost something central to the core of his being. We were not created to act like animals or to be ne'er-do-wells, but to have purpose and direction. We were created to need God. My connection to God through prayer is the way that I maintain a sense of wellbeing in my personal and professional life. This has been true for me through all the years, to the extent that I have told my wife, "If you hear me praying intensely, even in the middle of the night, please know that I just have to pray."

***Q: What is the greatest frustration you experience in doing this work, and what is the deepest satisfaction?***

PB: The most frustrating experience I have is when I meet people who are unconcerned about their spiritual development. Our level of interest, desire, and longing determines the amount of truth that we can perceive. If people knew to what degree they were affecting their spiritual growth by everything they do or don't do, they would assign more importance to their thoughts and actions. Many people do change their lives when they realize this, but there are those who are occupying their time on earth by distracting themselves from what they know—in their deepest hearts—they most need.

The most rewarding thing I experience is when people are open to receive the truth and then live it in the best way they can. It is very gratifying to get letters from people saying that they have followed through with information from a reading or workshop and have experienced promised results. My greatest reward is in knowing that a person has benefited from the truth that I could share.

I learned a long time ago that I don't teach anyone anything. I give information, which people can use to learn for themselves. No one ever teaches anyone anything, because we are only message bearers for each other. In that sense, I don't feel an attachment to outcomes for anyone, because I know that I am not responsible for causing another person to be or become anything.

I hope that in the future our organization, Adventures in Mastery, will have the chance to give information through educational programs that can liberate people by helping them learn how to enlighten themselves. Though we have no corner on the market of spiritual information, we have much knowledge and experience to share. We also have a very august spirit world, as exemplified by Saint Germain, and we have a history of consistency toward purpose. We are developing literature that will give people useful background information about the spirit world and spiritual growth.

# The Path of Spiritual Development

***Q: Most people do not have the spiritual experiences that you have had since childhood. How can people who are not mediumistic become aware of their spiritual senses?***

PB: Everyone has clairvoyance, clairaudience, and spiritual sensing because everyone is a spiritual being with the ability to become attuned to spirit. Many people perceive spirit without realizing it, as a message can come through a dream, a song that crosses the mind, or an unanticipated thought. Without adequate information or experience, people may even "get" the message and feel inspired, without recognizing that they have received communication from spirit.

A big factor in developing your spiritual senses is knowing whether or not it meets the longing of your heart. What do you long for in your life? For a job that pays more? For more children?

For a new car? Since the time of my earliest memory, what I longed for was to know God, so I started praying at a young age. Did I always know that God was there? I often felt the presence of God, but not all of the time. Whether or not I could know objectively that God was present, I felt a deep need for God, and that same longing is really in everyone. You just have to go deep enough within yourself to experience it. It is at that juncture, where you meet God within, that spiritual opening occurs almost without effort.

Spiritual opening also relates to a person's destiny and mission. I know that I was born to do this work, even though I came into it later in life, because everything up to that time was leading in this direction. I had to be born with certain natural skills in order to do what I am doing today. *Not everyone is destined to be a medium, but everyone is spiritual, and the essence of spirituality is love. Spend time applying the right principles and practicing love for yourself and others. Long to experience your own spirituality and your longing will open the door.*

One thing that helped me was that I read about the lives of the early saints, especially people like St. Francis. I realized that there was no limit to his positive imagining or his longing to be close to God. St. Francis was able to imitate Jesus not only because he read scriptures about him but also because he imagined Jesus clearly and longed to be like him. By doing this, he created a bond between himself and Jesus and had profound spiritual experiences with him.

If you believe you are trying and not progressing, it may be because your motivation is not deep enough. If you want a fire to burn brighter, with more heat and more light, you have to put more wood on it. For the flame of desire to grow, the kindling needed is to imagine the presence of God and long for that presence.

***Q: Can you talk about techniques to use to open our spiritual senses?***

PB: As I said, we can learn to recognize the messages of our guides and teachers in many ways, through thoughts, feelings, music, life events, or the words and actions of others, but one of the most direct ways is through a regular practice of meditation. In spiritual development classes, I have taught various meditation techniques, including the practice of beginning with prayer and the envisioning of being surrounded by light. This protects you as you enter a state of openness. Relaxation exercises can help you to go deeper into the meditative state. Another useful technique is to imagine a blank white movie screen. Without trying to see anything, you can watch the screen in your mind's eye until images appear, and words are spoken. In bookstores and libraries, there are excellent CDs with guided meditations that can assist you in your practice, especially in the beginning.

I tell students that the first thing to be aware of during meditation or any activity is that spirit speaks to you, *through* you. This is always true because God is the center of who you are. God's presence, love, intelligence, and wisdom dwell within you, and from that source comes the spiritual guidance you receive. If we are less highly developed in our spirituality, God speaks to us anyway, through our own conscience, and everyone has experienced that to a degree.

When you begin trying to receive from spirit, start by listening to your own inner voice. You need not take everything as guidance necessarily, but learn how to listen. People already do that unconsciously or subconsciously. If you consistently practice in this way, your guides and teachers will recognize this and come in on that frequency. They will come in on those occasions when you set the time aside to listen.

What I'm talking about is not unlike learning a language or learning to listen to another person. How do you enhance your ability to listen? You practice being attentive, focused, and clear in your intention. You let the other person know you're there and say what you want to talk about. The same skills are needed in communicating with spirit beings, because the spirit world and this world are the same in this regard. Communication is communication. To have better communication in either world, you need to clearly say what you want to talk about while you are with someone, and you need to listen actively when that person speaks.

One of your best tools can be journaling about your questions and allowing spirit to inspire the answers. Journaling objectifies your questions by placing them outside of yourself, rather than asking and listening only on the inner plane. It also captures your questions and answers on paper so that you can read them over. This doesn't mean that the first time you put pen to paper you are going to get a profound message, but unless a child takes the first step, she won't know how to take the second step. Through practice, you will see an increase in the quality of the content or the truth that is coming through, and you can begin to have confidence that spirit is speaking through you. Then more questions and more answers will come to you.

When I first tried journaling, I would write a question down so that I couldn't forget it, and then just sit and wait. I was taught that the first thought that comes through is what I should write down, and I learned not to second-guess myself. Even if you are receiving from yourself instead of spirit, if you find truth in what you write on paper it doesn't matter where it comes from. You are spirit also, and truth can come from you when you ask a question sincerely.

Whatever methods you choose, remember that good communication skills are important in interacting with spirit, just as they are in everyday life. If you practice any of these techniques regularly, your guides and teachers will meet you more than half way, and you can begin to have consistent encounters with them. Once this happens, you are less likely to feel the need for a spiritual reading, because you can make direct contact with God and with your own loving spirit guides and teachers. You are also engaged in the extraordinary adventure of learning to know your unfathomable self.

***Q: Can we, then, receive guidance from our own imagination as well as from spiritual sources, as long as we evaluate it to be sure it's beneficial?***

PB: In the end, yes. Information from any source should be considered on its merits. Doing this serves to protect you from being misguided or from applying guidance from a spirit who is less developed. If you find information coming through that is nonsense or just doesn't feel right, you obviously don't want to continue with that line of communication. Prayer before meditating or journaling will help to attract higher energies and discourage lower spirits from coming through. You can also pray for confirmation of guidance received, reflect on it as much as you need to, and discuss it with someone you trust before acting on it.

*Q:* ***If someone wants to become a medium like you, is it possible? What steps should be followed?***

PB: It's possible for a seriously interested person to become a medium. If you want to work professionally in this field, you need to know that you have a true calling and prepare yourself to work in a responsible fashion.

Where I grew up, relatives and neighbors of a family who had previously lived in our house were buried in a cemetery on our land that had many kinds of gravestones. One particular tombstone was in the shape of a pulpit with a Bible carved into the stone on top of it. As a little boy, I would climb up onto that stone and preach to whomever. I knew at that young age that I was called to do some kind of public spiritual work. Talking to a group about my spiritual experiences is as natural to me as breathing. I never get nervous speaking before audiences, no matter how many people are there. I'm not saying this to brag, but to show that I feel called to do this work. There are things I don't like to do that others are good at, but this work is something that comes naturally to me. The first thing to do is to ask yourself if you feel that you have this calling.

Be aware that there are lower entities, and don't try to do this alone. You do need to know what you are doing. For your own protection and the protection of those who trust you, prepare yourself by working with an experienced teacher. By doing this you will learn how to interact with the spirit world, how to see and hear spiritually, and how to know what it all means. When you study with an established professional medium as I did, you will receive much by osmosis, without having to go through every grade of the school of hard knocks. You may actually feel the calling more after you start studying with a teacher.

Another important step is to pray about this question. Really pray and ask to be guided. If you think you would like to do this kind of work, pray for forty days, three months, or however long you feel you need to pray. Ask God and spirit to impress you with what your next step should be. If you want to get a reading from me or from a medium of your choice as part of this guidance, do that, but be prepared to evaluate the information you receive that way.

I have to emphasize that being a medium is a big responsibility. Would I wish it on anyone else? Not really, unless you feel strongly guided to do this. Once you are committed, there is no real let-up. You have to stay focused and dedicated, continually doing your best to keep your mind and heart pure. I've taught people who are enthusiastic at the beginning but don't have staying power when they realize that the number-one prerequisite for successful mediumship is to be unselfish to the point of being sacrificial in the choices you make. You have to put God, the higher spirit world, and other people first.

You know, you only live once, so if you are determined to do something in life, don't leave any stone unturned. Don't stay in a job that you don't like, or one that you're not satisfied with. If you're not fulfilled or happy, ask the question, "*Why?*" If this field interests you, learn all you can about it. Invest yourself. You wouldn't buy a house sight unseen. You would go inside, examine the floor plan, walk through the house, and learn everything you could before you decide it is the right house for you. You should approach doing this work with the same care.

Prophets, mediums, psychics, soothsayers, and sages have existed throughout human history, and there will always be a need for them. God has used the relatively few people who can contact the spirit world directly to bring information through to individuals and even to the world. Such people have run the gamut from contacting lower to higher realms of the spirit world, but they have all had their place. For me personally, it is important to work for the highest possible spiritual purpose. This means that I have had to study, to be committed to serve God and others, and to live my own life with the greatest degree of love and purity that I can.

# Before Getting a Spiritual Reading

***Q:* *Can an inexperienced medium do more harm than good by giving clients subjective interpretations? Are there precautions for people wanting to get a spiritual reading?***

PB: When I am unavailable for a reading, people often ask if I can recommend someone, but I have learned that it is best not to give referrals. I may receive a good reading from a medium, and someone else may not. People do need to investigate before getting a reading, because inexperienced mediums have given misleading messages. Ask about the medium's credentials, and find out from those who have received a reading what their experience was like.

Can an inexperienced medium do more harm than good? If a person sits with any medium in a receptive state with a wide-open aura or energy field, whatever information is given will just pour in. More than one person who has had a reading with an inexperienced medium has been the victim of a careless word that has slipped deep into the heart and become an ongoing problem.

Years ago, I was on the Boardwalk in Atlantic City with Vivien, and we encountered a medium whose charge was ten dollars for a brief reading. On a lark, but half seriously, I decided to get a reading. One of the first things this person said to me was, "Well, I see that you are going to have a long life and that you will live to be eighty-six years old." I rarely tell people how long they're going to live, and only if *clearly* prompted by the spirit world, because once the mind is set on something, it can program itself to act out what it believes. We do that to ourselves all the time. Sometimes fears and phobias from childhood are not true, but we live as if they were. I am now more careful about choosing a medium, and I exercise my own judgment about what information is helpful to me and what is not.

***Q: How can a person receiving a reading best prepare to get a clear message from the spirit world?***

PB: I tell people to pray for the medium first, so that the medium can be properly open to the highest level of spirit and your spirit guides and teachers. Pray for compatibility between the medium and you, because that is the basis upon which spirit is able to come and work most fully. I always prepare to give a reading by praying for three days, not for any ritual purpose, but to create the right energy in me. Since the information will come through me, my energies have to be raised to a level that is harmonious with the higher energies of the spirit world. To prepare to receive a reading, you can meditate and reflect by going into your own heart and mind. Be very calm during the days before the reading so that you can be present without preconceptions or negative energy that could block your receiving the messages coming to you.

When I go to a medium for a reading, I have a positive and receptive attitude, but I'm very neutral, in terms of specific expectations. That is the best environment for a medium to be able to give information objectively and accurately. If they are not objective enough, it is possible for mediums to pick up the thoughts of clients and feed back to them what they want to hear. It is good to be neutral energetically during a reading and to wait until after the reading to evaluate the information.

***Q: If a person getting a reading is very skeptical or has many fears about the spirit world, does this affect a medium's ability to give accurate information?***

PB: Of course it does, because your attitude and energy influence the environment. The medium's attitude is also important. Everything is energy, and if you introduce fear, you will repel high-level spirits and positive energy. If you have such concerns, it is important to pray and ask to be at peace. This will help if you really want or need to get a reading, but you are feeling fearful. What you give out is what you get back. I have had a reading myself when I have not felt at peace, either in the environment, with the medium, or with myself, and I didn't get a good reading under those conditions.

That said, some mediums are so experienced, objective, and at such a level that they are not affected by anything a client brings in. Still, the spirit world vibrates at the same frequency as the energy that is built between the person coming for a reading and the medium. If that energy is inharmonious and not at a high enough frequency, it will affect the kind of information that comes through. The highest information will be blocked, or the client will not be able to receive it. Energetically speaking, this is a scientific reality.

***Q: What actually happens during a reading? What do you see and hear with your spiritual senses?***

PB: I have developed instructions to help clients prepare for readings, so they usually come with questions that are important to them at this time in their lives. When I give a reading, each client's guides and my own guides spiritually prepare the environment. Prayer before the reading contributes to the elevated atmosphere that can exist during a reading. Having prepared before the reading, I have already entered a semitrance state, and I can see each person's life in front of me, often including the past, present, and future. I open each session with prayer, and the prayer itself is often influenced by what I am beginning to see and feel. My guides and teachers move around me, and the person's guides and teachers are present. They all help to bring in the information.

I mentioned to you earlier that one of my guides is Kathryn Kuhlman, the great faith healer who first came into my life appearing as a little guide using the name Tiffany. I walked into a bookstore one day and read that the name

Tiffany means "God's appearance." Kathryn Kuhlman comes to me in dreams and provides many details during the readings I give for people. She is a powerful individual who brings through much information.

My guides often communicate by placing pictures in front of me that relate to a client's concerns. If a person has a question about marriage, Tiffany will put a gold ring in front of me. If it's about a conflict in a marriage, I may see a husband and wife in a boxing ring. Various symbols are used repeatedly to indicate a certain situation or issue. It is a part of the gift of mediumship to be able to see and interpret such symbols. While they appear in a flash, the longer I work as a medium, the longer my guides hold these symbols and the longer they stay visible. Central to the readings I give are the messages that come through my channeling Saint Germain. He speaks directly to clients about their deeper questions, sometimes at length.

At the end of a reading, I experience that the energies are waning and that the spirits who have come to speak are pulling back. Almost always, both the client and I feel a deep sense of gratitude, and I close each reading with prayer.

*Q: Many who have readings from you say that their lives change for the better, and they want to receive additional readings. Why do you think that happens?*

PB: I hear this all the time, and I'm greatly humbled by it, because I feel as though I'm something like a translator for the United Nations, simply giving what I receive. Of course, a medium with certain qualifications has to be in place, but on the whole, I give what is given to me.

From what my clients tell me, they are deeply comforted to know that deceased loved ones are still alive in the spirit world, speaking to them from a place of greater love and wisdom. They also express that they receive important guidance about how to handle situations in their daily lives relating to work, children, health, or other important issues.

The reason people say that their lives change for the better is not only because of the information that comes through, but also because of an essential change that can occur energetically. To the extent that they are receptive to it, people receive healing energy, love, and wisdom from the higher realms of spirit that becomes a literal part of who they are. They become aware that they are not alone and never have been. They realize that they are constantly being shepherded by loving spiritual guides and teachers and by the abiding presence of God. This may not happen for everyone who has a reading, but I have received this kind of feedback so often that I know without a doubt that it is true for many.

# Questions for Our Time

***Q: You have had extensive communication with the spirit world. Has this given you insight into the causes of war and other negative behaviors among human beings?***

PB: That's a big question. The spirit world has a greater influence on our world than most people realize. I believe what Saint Germain has told me—that the basic purpose of my work is to help people find God within and to grow spiritually—but people also need to know about how the spirit world interacts with us while we are on earth. As long as we don't know, we're victims of our ignorance, and this works strongly against humanity in winning spiritual freedom.

The overshadowing of individuals and humanity as a whole by darker energies is very real, and I have met those forces. There are people on earth and in the spirit world who have made very limited spiritual progress, and they still love to see other people suffer. Much evil comes from jealousy, which arises because people are envious of what others have. When people feel covetous, they want to destroy the happiness of others because they are not happy. That is a frequent basis for negative behaviors on earth and for the attraction of lower spirits to individuals and to the planet. Some spirits come because of blind ignorance or fury.

People who spent much of their lives on earth with no spiritual content may not realize that they have died. They are not malevolent—just ignorant. They hang around the earth plane until they finally understand the truth about their situation and move on. That is why some houses and graveyards are haunted. Such people may be so attached to the earth that they don't seem to be able to evolve spiritually.

Mental hospitals are filled with people who have been diagnosed as suffering from schizophrenia and other psychiatric disturbances. Science has discovered organic causes for some mental illnesses but has not recognized that earthbound or negative spirits can influence patients. Much suffering results from this. Medical and mental health professionals are able to help people understand how the brain, mind, and emotions work, but until the phenomena of spirit influence is understood as an objective reality, there will be some patients who can be helped to cope, but not overcome.

As for war, there are people on earth who are warlike, and they feel justified in creating conflict and human suffering in order to achieve their ends. They draw to themselves the same kind of warring spirits, including people who were warriors on earth, such as any number of Roman dictators who ordered thousands of people into battle. Some people in leadership roles on earth may be so overshadowed by warrior spirits that they become irrational enough to use their roles to carry out war or warlike measures. Peacemakers draw spirits of peace, warlike people draw spirits of war, and there are all shades between these two extremes.

In a very real sense, when we are in conflict with another, we are in conflict with ourselves. By going within to meet God, we begin to experience that God lives within everyone on earth and that we are all connected to each other by the energy of universal love and wisdom. War is a result of our ignorance of God's presence within all beings. When we understand and experience God's love within ourselves, within the physical universe, and within each person we meet, we will begin to experience peace. Peace can only be expressed in the world by those who know it within themselves.

***Q: From your perspective as a medium, what is the relationship between spiritual experiences and religion?***

PB: What is the true purpose of religion? It is a means, not an end, and it exists to help us draw closer to God. Most great religions include elevated teachings and spiritual practices, such as prayer and meditation, which ultimately result in the opening of our spiritual senses. Prophets of old saw visions and received messages for the people from the spirit world. On a "mountain apart" (traditionally Mount Tabor), three disciples of Jesus, Peter, James, and his brother John, clairvoyantly saw Moses and Elijah appear in spirit and converse with Jesus. Based on his own deep prayer and meditation, St. Francis had profound mystical experiences that led him to ecstasy with God. Joan of Arc had visions and heard voices. The traditions of every great religion describe mystical practices that move people beyond their belief systems to have direct experiences with God. Spiritual experience is an integral part of religious experience.

Religion has played a divisive role in human history whenever people have used it as justification for domination and even destruction of others. This is clearly a misuse of religion and a distortion of its true purpose.

From my experience over all the years of being a medium, I have come to believe that there is one true religion—the religion of love. There is one true mystical experience, and that is the direct experience of God within. From those things flow outer manifestations such as heartfelt religious practice, true community, and service to others. In that way, people should feel free to follow the faith of their choice or follow an independent spiritual path. The reality of God within each human being is a unifying experience available to all who seek it, regardless of what worldview or religion they embrace.

***Q: Does each person on earth have spirit guides and teachers? If so, what is their role with us?***

PB: Each of us has spiritual guides, teachers, and guardian angels who are assigned to us at birth. Some of them remain with us all of our lives, but changes can occur as we ourselves change and grow. If we begin to specialize in a task on earth, it could be because we are being guided in that direction. We might then draw to ourselves teachers from the spirit world who have expertise in that area.

We usually have a master teacher who coordinates the guidance we receive. A guide may play the role of protector and gatekeeper in relation to other spirits. Various guides may help us with work, emotional, or health concerns. However, the overarching goal of spirit is to help us to know ourselves, to know God, and to express God's love in the world.

The earth experience is our school, and physical energy is important for growing spiritually. We learn about ourselves through relating to other people, and that is the *summum bonum,* or greatest good, of this earthly life. By helping us to grow while we are on earth, our spirit guides and teachers move with us to higher spiritual levels. My guides, including Saint Germain, have reminded me more than once that they do not wish to be thought of as apart from humanity. They are as human as we are, and they know firsthand what our life experience on earth is like. The elevated energy that we often feel when they are near is something we ourselves can realize.

When we know that we are surrounded by loving spiritual beings who fully understand us and have our highest good at heart, we need never feel alone again. When we are celebrating, they rejoice with us. When we are discouraged, lonely, or sad, they are there to comfort us. Throughout our lives, they move closest to us in times of physical or emotional suffering. They whisper in our ear that we are loved, that all is not lost, and that this too will pass.

I know from experience that spirit guides and teachers are real. As a spiritual teacher and medium, I am aware that teachers in spirit work with me and through me on an ongoing basis. I constantly interact with spirits and angels who descend night and day, moving between the physical and spiritual worlds.

God also uses the angelic world and the spiritual world to help the earth to evolve, and people's knowledge of this reality is increasing. There are many mediums today, and there is a growing prevalence of meditation among individuals and groups.

This wave of spirituality has come to the earth plane because of intense input from the spirit world. Elevated spiritual beings are inspiring people and moving us in this direction. Many people are talking about a great shift in consciousness within humanity. All of this is happening because hordes of spirits are descending to earth with the great message that each person is a spiritual being who never dies. We have known this as a theory, but many now experience this directly, in a way that transcends religion, or even thought.

***Q: Can you tell us something about the spirit world, and what we will experience when we die?***

PB: Because God is love, there is no end to love or life. Heaven is not a place, but a state of being; and if we graduate correctly from the earth plane, we go into a spiritual state that includes endless levels of learning and love. Spiritual masters such as Jesus, Buddha, Saint Germain, and others like them are in the highest realms of heaven. Those who have lived good lives are in realms reflecting their level of growth. People who are completely unprepared for the reality of the spirit world may initially experience confusion. Those who have harmed others or spent time with negative thoughts and behaviors are in the lowest realms, and there is every degree in between. We go where our love takes us, and in that sense judgment is always self-imposed.

Each of us is already a spirit. When our physical bodies die, we simply move away from them, leaving behind every material thing we have owned. We still have form, though it vibrates at a much higher frequency than our dense physical bodies, and we can no longer be seen or heard through the physical senses of those still alive on earth.

After being oriented by guiding spirits or going through a time of healing if we have been ill, we can soon have full and busy lives on the other side. Everything we see is flooded with energy, color, and beauty that is much more vivid and real than anything we experience on earth with our limited physical senses. The homes, environments and, yes, the neighbors surrounding us in eternity perfectly reflect the level of love and understanding we have reached in this life. Because love is energy that has its own frequency level, we arrive in a realm where the frequency exactly matches that of our own spirit. We would not feel comfortable anywhere else.

Unless we experience God on earth, not as an intellectual or religious concept, but in reality, it is unlikely that we will find ourselves close to God in the spirit world. That is why it is important to search for spirituality while we are on earth. We can find it most directly through meditation but also by honoring the presence of God in ourselves, in others, and in nature.

The spirit world is vaster than we can comprehend. Regardless of where we are when we enter it, we can continue to advance to higher levels through our work in the spirit world, by helping others still on earth, and by accepting the assistance of loving spirits from realms higher than our own.

If you wish to know where you will be when you arrive in the spirit world, look back on your life so far. If you can feel at peace, you have probably lived a good life and can positively answer the questions, "Who am I? Have I been truthful? What kind of a character do I have? Have I loved others unselfishly? What has been the chief object of my love?" If you are honest with yourself, you will know, not exactly, but you will know enough.

***Q: Some mediums channel predictions, messages about extraterrestrials or other ideas beyond our common experience. How do we decide what to believe about such information?***

PB: Discernment always occurs in relationship to your level of spiritual development. If something is beyond your reach in knowledge, understanding, or experience and has no apparent relevance to your life, you don't need to make it part of your walk at this point. Know yourself, know where you are, and trust yourself, remembering that you are also being guided by your teachers in spirit. It is kind to listen and good to consider new ideas, but if something is not attractive to you and doesn't speak to you, that is a sign that it is probably not for you right now. Maybe a UFO will land in your back yard tomorrow and awaken you to the reality of UFOs, but until then, they may not be so applicable to your life.

You may receive information that contains some truth, but it is not from the highest level of spirit. You may encounter great truth and not be ready for it, just as a first grader is not ready for the fifth grade. If you are concerned about a particular teaching or experience, you can pray and ask, never doubting that you will be led by kind and wise guides and by God. One good rule of thumb to follow is that if a teaching doesn't lift you up, and you don't feel attracted to it, you can leave it alone. It is probably not the right direction for you at this time. Respect your own life experience and spiritual development and continue your walk in joy.

***Q: Is there anything else about your life or about being a medium that you want to share with people?***

PB: Whether or not you become a medium is not the point. The point is that God is real. Where is God? As much as I can discern, and from ancient and modern teachings that I embrace, I can tell you that God is within each one of us. Jesus indicated that when he said, "The Father and I are one." Because we are so earth-oriented, we do not know our true inner reality. When you meditate regularly and go inside, you rise up from the common world to the superconscious mind. There you will find God. You will find your own highest self. When Saint Germain called this higher self the *I AM* presence, he was talking about the same thing.

If you do nothing else in life, whether or not you pursue mediumship, learn to meditate. Go inside and find God. That is ultimately why you exist. I would say to everyone, the world without you would not be complete. You are one of the unique pieces in the puzzle of humanity, so more than your career or the acquisition of things, the important thing is to know yourself. When you know yourself, you will come to have great patience, compassion, and deep love for yourself. If I have learned anything, it is that. It was a lesson hard won.

In all of my searching and in serving others, I was so busy that I forgot to take care of myself. Saint Germain was instrumental in showing me that there were levels within that I had not looked at. He did not mean negative areas, but levels that would be beneficial to me and to many. He asked me to look, really look, within myself and said, "In love, we never give up; we never condemn." When I finally looked within, I saw many levels that made me appreciate myself.

After this experience, I stopped criticizing and finding fault with myself because of my mistakes, ineptitude, or short-comings. I could totally relax, and with that, I was liberated. I encourage you to do the same thing. Look within, without fear of what you will find. You will find truth, which includes your mistakes and areas where you need to change and grow, but if you see yourself with compassion and continue to look, ever more deeply, you will find vast untapped resources of love and wisdom. You will find God.

# Part II
# Wisdom of Spirit

*Questions and Answers with Saint Germain*

*Channeled by Philip Burley*

# Wisdom of Spirit

# Introduction by Saint Germain

I AM REALLY HERE WHEN I speak through Philip. It is not good acting but soul-to-soul oneness. If I were completely in him, I could animate his entire body and even cause him to get up and walk, but Philip is not that kind of medium. We are not concerned about spiritual phenomena but the truth that comes through. May it touch your heart and mind and change the direction of your life, if need be. I am deeply pleased that many people today appreciate the spiritual side of life and thus strive toward perfection in terms of living correctly. As our hearts meet, I can feel that you are longing for spiritual perfection and for freedom from want, worry, doubt and insecurity. In that longing, we become one.

I do not come alone but as one of a number of masters representing the divine order and a certain aspect of the totality of God. What I bring is different from the emanations of other masters but not apart from them. I come mostly in gold and purple light, which is a radiation of energy at the highest level, having to do with nobility—things of the spirit, soul, and God. Because I come out of the center of love to bring God's presence, you will feel the vibration of warmth, kindness, and love that comes from spirit, and it will help you to recognize the truth that I bring. Whether you believe in me or not, I believe in you, and I am here for the very special purpose of bringing divine love.

## *My Work*

I am a universal being and I work with humanity worldwide. I am interested in all who seek to live the truth and to raise their love and awareness to a higher level. When I channeled information through Mr. Guy Ballard in the last century, I emphasized the *I AM* teachings, and some of what I said was cloaked in words that were not easily understood. My work today is an extension of that work, but it is at a higher, deeper level. Because humanity has advanced, I can say more now than I have ever said before, and this is very gratifying for me. I have been working for eons of time to come to the point where I can speak fully and completely about God. Through this instrument and others around the world, I am teaching one most important idea: that each one must work with the cause of life, not just the effect.

My work is inner work. If you asked me about a specific belief such as reincarnation, I would say little, because I am speaking to *everyone* about this inner work, not only to those who do or do not believe in reincarnation.

## *Channeling through Philip*

The first indication that we can use someone as a channel is consistency toward purpose, and the second is obedience. The great ones who have come into full God-realization and self-realization are those who surrendered themselves to God. Philip was prepared from childhood to be a channel for spirit, and my meeting with him was no accident. Before I stepped fully into his life, I tested him more than once, and he tested me. Like many mediums, he did not accept all of this without questioning. He finally understood that his mediumship was authentic after he had many validating experiences on his own as well as meaningful testimonies from other mediums.

Coming to certain mediums is like coming to a busy shopping mall at lunch hour where there is only one telephone booth, and hundreds of people want to get on the phone. When I speak through Philip, a host of masters and angels from the spirit world surrounds us, operating behind the scenes. Thousands of spirits gather to learn and grow, observing the channeling phenomenon so they can work with individuals on earth with greater understanding. They draw upon the energy of those who have come seeking truth, not in an exploitive way, but in love.

When I speak through Philip, I listen attentively to individuals who have gathered to hear me, and I look to see how they are touched spiritually. Some think that they are doing all of the work and thinking all of their thoughts, but the masters work together behind the scenes to inspire them in many ways. What is important is that people *are* touched spiritually, and that they are not the same as they were before this experience. They take some spiritual element with them that makes them richer.

## *Life is a Search for Self and God*

In this life course, even though you have friends and relatives, you come in and go out as an individual. One of the lonely things about finding higher knowledge is that you cannot really share it with others who have not yet reached the same point. Some of your walk will be lonely, but that is a part of the price of realizing the fullness of what and who you are.

People everywhere are trying to find themselves. Your whole life search, everything you do, and all you go through, is about that. Whether or not you learn the answers to your specific questions is less important than realizing yourself. As it is said, when you truly find yourself, you find God, and when you truly find God, you find yourself. Then, by the transcendent spiritual positioning of yourself, you find the answers to all of your questions.

Dear friends, what you most deeply seek can be perceived only in the superconscious or transcendent state. Some of you know about this, and others have experienced it. Books may enhance your walk by pointing the way, but all the knowledge in the world will not give you what you long for. Only life experience can teach you to awaken to your higher self, to truly know what this life is about by seeing it from the mountaintop. Why? Because the kingdom of heaven is within you. God is within.

Each of you is a soul, living in the form of a physical body, and at the core, each of you is a pinpoint of light—a projection of the creator. As you trace your life force, the light within you, back to its source, you will find that we all emanate from one reservoir of endless, love-filled, and eternal light that is God. The creative principle is the essence of God, who loved what he perceived in his own mind. The wonder of this is that God could project himself out to enjoy and appreciate his own beauty and creativity. Out of the yearning to see and know himself, out of absolute necessity, God created all things. You, dear ones, were the last of creation, the ones for whom everything else was created.

God is invisible and infinite, yet finite through you. God perceives and appreciates each time that you perceive and appreciate the smallest to the largest created thing. God belongs to people who live this way. When you are thankful, not just for the things that you have, but for each created thing, you will experience the element of love. This is truly what each of us is longing for, and it is what I am longing to bring to earth.

The highest understanding is the truth of all truths: You came from God. You are one and the same. You are God—indivisible, absolute and supreme. When you come to that knowledge, not in theory, but through experience, you are liberated from ignorance and from lesser truth that you may have embraced. If you ask any of the masters what the hallmark of their breakthrough was, they would say, "I came to realize I am God. I am not different from God." That was the final step. You came from God, as God to earth, to live out the life you are living, to go through the process of searching and finding. The longing that everyone feels is the longing to find self. No matter what else you may think, the soul's longing is always to find self.

## *Invest Yourself*

The most important revelation and revolution are in you. The teachings I have brought, or that anyone has brought, find value when you take them in and make them your own, eat them up, and incorporate them *consciously* into your daily life. When you do something halfheartedly, you get half the results, so invest yourself. The masters, guides, and teachers who are working with you know exactly what they are doing, so when you are on the path, pursue completely the good that you find in front of you. This will take you to the next step, and the next step and the next step.

You are on earth in this body because you are a student, not because you are a graduate. Don't you want to graduate from earth? Would you not like to come where I am, where there is perpetual light, love, and freedom? I must emphasize what is often the missing link in a person's ability to come to God: You must turn inward to find self, to find unconditional love, and to find God.

Use your life energy to fulfill your own personal mission of self-integration and self-realization in order to feel at peace as you look back on your life. If you do not do this, you will feel less satisfied, even if you have worked on the outer plane to benefit others. Many great and powerful leaders, whose actions have influenced thousands, were wanting in spirit when they were ready to pass on. This is because they did not climb the ladder of inner life. They did not meditate upon the inner plane and seek to arrive at a direct experience with the living God within. They did not see their own spirits, their own light. They did not awaken to the fact that they are God, that they are one and the same.

Some people live for many years on earth and never look at the stars, the planets or the moon. They never have one bit of curiosity to look up and out, and they die that way. You have to be hungry for spiritual growth in order to realize it. You have to be willing to roll back the old to make room for the new, and to climb higher and higher within yourself.

I come in order to point the way and to encourage you. Follow the dictates of your own heart, but continue to try to go beyond where you are. Challenge yourself to gain higher knowledge, higher truth, higher understanding and greater love.

## Spirit of Adventure

The Spirit of God in you enjoys the sport of adventure, so you are given a script to live out. Though you experience the adventures and the challenges of life, remember that there is only one source, one energy, and one will. Until you attain a higher level of consciousness, it will appear that you have total free will, but your life is being guided by a higher presence. Call it God, divine will, or divine love. In the end, everything will come out for your greatest good, because that is who God is. Enjoy the challenges and the adventure, but live with right thinking, right action, and right associates.

When you live in duality it appears otherwise, but in your soul of souls, as you ascend into the higher self, you will experience the truth that there is one energy, one light, one intelligence, and that you are but a projection of that reality. To experience this as reality, you have to live out your life. When you read a book, the author does not mean for you to stop and say, "Hey, this is just a book! These characters aren't real. They are just created out of the mind of the author!" No, the author sells many books because through the imagination, the reader enters into the lives of the characters and can't put the book down. That's how this life is. You have to live it out, because it's what is playing on your screen. It is the book of your life, and it is what is unfolding for you. Enjoy the book! Enjoy the movie!

## We Meet You Where You Are

We in spirit are helping a broad array of people on earth who have all kinds of understandings, concepts, and belief systems. We must approach each of you where you are and according to your beliefs, myths and fears. Wherever you are, dear ones, we meet you in kindness and love. Like parents, we approach you with the deepest of care, as if you were ourselves, never to criticize or judge. Even if you have an extreme or unusual belief, we speak to you in your own terms and lead you within your belief system. We know that you will gradually come to a greater understanding, sometimes through pain and suffering, and you will say, "Ah, there is a higher truth. There is more that I need to learn, and there is wisdom beyond what I know."

If you see yourself as less advanced than someone else on the path, don't envy that person. You will advance as you will advance. It is all part of the great unfolding of God's will on the earth plane for you. You may feel that there is too much to absorb, understand, and apply. Learn and apply what you can, and don't be intimidated. If there is something that you don't agree with, meditate, wait, and see. You may not accept everything that you read or hear, and that's life. It is a part of what is needed for your own individual growth. Sometimes you are ready to awaken to certain truths, and sometimes you are not.

Anyone on the path of spiritual growth, at whatever level, will serve themselves well by being very patient, because spiritual advancement cannot be pushed. Why? Because your growth takes what it takes. You have to go through what you have to go through to balance the scale so that you may reach perfection. Without that, there would be no justice. Every person, without exception, must go through their own experiences of growth by falling down and getting up, taking wrong turns to take right turns, going down the wrong fork in the road to find the right fork, and misunderstanding to understand better.

*There is no such thing as being off your path.* Wherever you are at any one moment, *is* your path. Where you are in a moment does not always agree with your idea of how life should be, and you think that there is some mistake. No, there is something for you to learn from that experience, and once you have learned it you will move on. Where you find yourself after that is also your path. Even if it doesn't appear to be so, you are where you belong. Just remember that the path is the means, and not the end. Celebrate the means and squeeze everything you can out of your present experience. Gain all the understanding you can. Pay attention to whatever appears before you.

## *Which Way is Right for You?*

There is great diversity both in the spiritual goals of each person and in the methods that can be used to achieve those goals. My rule of thumb is this: If you are not attracted by an idea, you can let it go. You would not buy a piece of clothing that did not attract you. If an idea attracts you after you have examined it long enough, it is probably for you. More than likely, it *is* for you.

When Philip first allowed me to come through him, he did much questioning as to whether or not he wanted to do mediumship work. When he saw that such work would allow him to aid his own soul's evolution and help others at the same time, he said, "Let's do it." From then on, I worked with him with great dedication as he applied himself to the task.

Remember that beliefs can be roadblocks rather than doors, so it behooves us to keep examining what we believe with an open mind and an open heart. This is the means by which we become advanced souls. In my effort to climb the ladder of life while on earth, I was confronted by new realizations many times. Because I was earnest, I would question and doubt, leaving no stone unturned until I was shown a new level of truth. In that way, I discovered higher wisdom and liberated myself.

## *Meditation*

In the process of spiritual discovery, meditation is imperative. Many of you may already meditate. It is a key practice, so don't give up on it. Meditation leads us into the light within each person, and that light imparts healing power and love. You may begin by breathing in deeply and focusing on your breath. Breath is life. As you continue to focus, ground yourself to the center of Mother Earth. As we affectionately pull you toward us, you will be suspended in the energy of our love between heaven and earth.

Meditation is like placing pieces of typing paper on a table. At first, the stack is not very high, but if you continue to place one piece on top of another, you will have fifty, one hundred, or even one thousand pieces of paper. The stack will build up until you are moving toward a spiritual breakthrough, with higher and higher realizations. This level of spiritual perception is possible because of God within, so where do you have to go? I will say again and again, go *inside*. Climb the stairs through thoughtful, consistent, deeply penetrating meditation. If you do that, you will find many of the answers you seek.

Originally, people were naturally spiritually open. Guided by the angelic world, they knew that the pathways of life were on the inner plane as well as on the outer plane, and they could easily go inside to ask questions. They would move through their chakras or spiritual energy vortices to increasingly elevated levels of energy until they found themselves in the midst of the radiation and vibration of the seventh, or crown, chakra. Through this natural practice, they attained spiritual awakening through direct and complete contact with God. They came fully into their God presence and found self. That was the original ideal and the original experience. It is important to understand your own spiritual anatomy, so that you can re-establish your connection with your God-centered self and continue your spiritual quest.

## Love Others Unconditionally

For me the word God is a verb. Yes, a noun, but also a verb, because God is manifested through love, and love is expressed not through passivity but through action. If you love someone, you may say, "I love you," which is a form of action, but a better way to show love is to really hug the person, serve the person, or give a gift. My way of drawing people is to love them unconditionally. Ultimately, this kind of love brings salvation to each of us, and it is the means to overcome the lack of ability to forgive.

When Philip asked me how he could help me come closer to him, I said, "Strengthen unselfish love within yourself. Whether or not you like what a person does, love that person just as he is. If you'll do that, it will bring me so close to you that I will become permanently cemented into your aura, and we will move together at all times." We have been doing that for more than twenty-one years, and he has faithfully walked this walk.

Love people unconditionally, no matter who they are or what they do to you or others. See each person as yourself and not as separate from you, and your spiritual guides and teachers will be drawn very close to you. You will grow very fast, and you will not have to deal so much with the psychology of overcoming.

# Questions and Answers with Saint Germain

# Spiritual Growth and Understanding

***Q: What are the most important steps we can take to ensure the soul's optimal growth in this lifetime?***

SG: The first and most important thing you can do is to love yourself as you are, and don't try to change yourself to conform to someone else's ideas of who or what you should be. The truth is what matters. Do you remember the teaching that truth will set you free? Love yourself as you are and do not pretend to be different from what you are. I don't mean that you should tell everyone your faults and shortcomings, because that is between you and God; but loving yourself just as you are is the beginning of being able to learn and grow. We will meet you where you are, in order to take you where you need to be.

In spite of the many religions, teachers, gurus and masters that have existed in the world, things don't seem to change much. Why is this so? Though truth has been known and practiced by some, humankind as a whole has not learned that God exists in each one, and that each one is literally the temple of God. Know that you are a great being. To love yourself properly, you must learn how to go inside and discover the light that you are.

You may recognize the presence of God through the still, small voice speaking within you, but to experience knowing God directly, deep inside your soul, you must raise your vibration. You have to move away from the physical frequency into the spiritual frequency through meditation. Going inside will cause you to be in a meditative state without even trying.

Even those who are infirm and cannot move can enter a state that is removed from ordinary consciousness. An awareness, impression, dream, insight or vision floats into their minds and causes them gradually to shift into higher consciousness. Being on this path is innate to every human soul. God planted within each of you the hunger, drive, and desire to know higher and higher truth and you cannot avoid it. Your life circumstances, whatever they may be, will motivate you to search higher and deeper.

***Q: Can you suggest tools to help us remember who we truly are?***

SG: Remember to remember! It is that simple. Who is going to do that for you if you don't do it for yourself? Keeping a journal, over many years, is a means for you to chart your course. Your guides and teachers in spirit can also use it as a tool to lead you. Keep track of each step of your life on paper. Write down your experiences in meditation and other important milestones in your spiritual journey. Your journals will become a resource for you over time. I have spoken through Philip and to him in his journals, and he has used them as a basis for books he has written.

If you want to remember something specific, such as a regular time for meditation or prayer, write yourself a note and put it where you are sure to see it. Remembering is your responsibility. Find your own method, but invest yourself in remembering to remember, day by day.

Each of you has your own individual door that only *you* can open and walk through. Jesus said to ask, seek and knock. You have to knock, turn the knob and walk through your door. On the other side of it are all the answers you have ever wanted in life. To become your true self and realize completely who you really are is a matter of being earnest in your search to know the heart of God. One day at a time, you will come to know that you make God happy in you, and you will become happy in God. People cannot truly find themselves and fulfill their lives to the utmost degree without finding God within. I have said it many times, and I will say it forever.

***Q: How can we enhance our creativity?***

SG: If you could see this world from our point of view, you would shift around many things, and your life could then run more smoothly. You would see the areas where you are wasting time that have nothing to do with eternity.

Creativity is God. It is the basis of his being. Creativity is one of the major realities of God. Otherwise, God could not have created what he imagined. God contains all things, and from all that he discerned within himself, which is everything, God imagined. What he imagined came from his whole being, and through his imagination, he projected out what he was imagining. Creativity and imagination are two sides of the same coin. Use your imagination to go deep within yourself to learn how you can become more creative.

The things you need in your life are waiting for you. God is not a Scrooge. He is not at all selfish. He is a cornucopia of everything, waiting to pour out to you. The problem is that you don't ask deeply enough. You can shorten your time on the path by becoming more imaginative, more creative, and asking with greater earnestness. Imagination is the path, the key, and the door to the spirit world. The kind of discernment that you want does not come from earth, but from heaven.

In times of emergency or in times of seeking faster progress, it may be necessary to sacrifice parts of your existence to support others, but in general, it is best to maintain a balance in life. This balance is determined on a case-by-case basis, hour by hour, and day by day. You may believe that creativity is something extemporaneous, but it is good to have structure in your life, including daily meditation and prayer. You may not do it 365 days a year because you are too tired, or other things come up, but generally, it is beneficial to follow structure and discipline.

The development of the creative art of mediumship, for example, is enhanced when life has a structure, rather than when it comes only through the overshadowing of a person by a spirit. You need training to know how to raise your vibration so that you draw in only the highest and best energy. Disciplines such as prayer and meditation can create the structure by which a high spiritual teacher can come to you, or through you.

You draw to yourself what you are, so spiritual masters and teachers in music and art often overshadow people who are engaged in such creative work. Even those of you who do counseling may suddenly get an insight because you are inspired by a teacher or guide with knowledge in that field. The answers come to you, and after a while, you begin to hear the independent voice of a spirit who is helping you with your work.

Invite spirit into your life to enhance your creativity, but be sure that you offer yourself as a proper vehicle, by attending to all aspects of your life.

*Q: Why do good people have lives filled with suffering, sometimes from childhood through adulthood?*

SG: Among those who have seen the spirit world, few have looked into the *highest* realms where ultimate causes of effects on earth are perfectly known. God is omniscient and omnipresent, knowing the past, present and future, but the future is usually hidden from you on earth so that you encounter challenges as though you have never faced them before. If you know what is coming ahead of time, how can you be tested and come to know your own strengths and weaknesses? Facing challenges that you do not anticipate is how you grow in strength and character—how you discover your true self and God.

Depending on how you respond to suffering, it does or does *not* have value. Throughout your life, you are meant to move gradually to higher and higher levels, but when you do not learn from your suffering, it is as though you are walking in circles. You do not go higher until your response to suffering changes. As many teachers have correctly said, it is not what happens to us that matters, but how we respond to it.

In no way do I minimize the need for compassion for people who suffer. Many suffer because of ignorance of the principles of which I speak. The reason that spirit is coming to earth in the way I am doing now is so that we may personally awaken you to the fact that we exist. We want to reach those who do not know about spirit, those who have never experienced us, so that we may impart these truths. Once people understand these principles, they can become self-evident and most helpful. Once you understand, you can wake up and stop walking in circles. You can go higher and higher until there is no more to undo. Then your suffering ends.

***Q:* *It is especially hard to see our own children and grandchildren suffer. How can we come to accept this, and how can we help?***

**SG:** Teach your children and grandchildren about their true selves. Jesus taught that he was the temple of God, saying, "He who has seen me has seen the Father," and "The Father and I are one." How did Jesus come to discern these realities? He meditated for hours and hours, learning from the masters how to meditate at the deepest level until he experienced his divine, limitless self—an ocean of light and love in which he saw all things contained—but at the same time, he remained in an earthly body. He had to live out the script that he had been given, and he was caught between his divinity, as demonstrated in miracles and prophecy, and his humanity.

As you know, Jesus suffered greatly. Because he was not the son of Joseph, he looked different from his brothers and sisters, so they mocked and shunned him. This was also part of the script he was given. To find solace from such injustices, and to find the very truth of heavenly things, Jesus prayed and meditated ardently throughout his short life. As a result of coming into such fine attunement to God, Jesus discovered his own divinity. This divine inner reality was the source of his ability to perform miracles, deliver healing energy to others, and ultimately to be resurrected to stand in full spiritual stature as the brightest light in the spirit world up to that point. Those of you who have a relationship with Jesus can ask him if what I have told you is true. He will say yes.

Through the example of Jesus and others, we learn that suffering is part of the path to enlightenment and self-discovery. You can see this in your own life and in the lives of people of your generation who sustain physical and emotional injuries. Some of them become greatly elevated people, serving as role models of grace, compassion, and strength, as they overcome their challenges and reach out to help others. If your children and grandchildren face obstacles, teach them to use their suffering toward constructive and positive ends, to be examples, and to help others.

***Q: Sometimes the spirit is still loving and wanting to serve, but the body becomes old and decrepit. Would you speak to this issue?***

SG: I understand your consternation, but you are where you are according to the one divine will. There are certain things that you experience at this age, such as growing into a desire for greater self-mastery and liberation, which you did not experience when you were younger. Take it all in with gratitude, and your suffering will be shortened. You will be enlightened. Many times we resist change, not just because we don't like it, but because we're not open to it at a deep enough level. Many truths and positive changes could come quickly to humanity if people could receive them with open hearts and open arms.

People said that I, Saint Germain, never aged, and that I discovered the elixir of life. That is partly true, but the greatest elixir of life is positive thinking. That will keep you younger than all the elixirs, creams, or massages in the world. You have to be young from the inside out to be young from the outside in.

When you are a master with fully opened spiritual senses, you may go deeper into the recesses of yourself to examine yourself, ask questions, and discern the truth about yourself. The greatest truth is you. The most important person to love and to know is you. People have it backward who think, "I should just reach out more, love more, and give more to others." There is truth in that idea, but first you have to become an instrument that has the ability to do that. The tree that does not send its roots down into fertile soil to receive nutrients and water cannot bear fruit. You have to put yourself in the right place and in the right circumstances. This begins to happen when you have the right attitude.

I feel your sadness about aging, in light of what you have learned and what you long for, but remember that God is wise, and it's not over until it's over. There may be some very big, good surprises ahead of you. Keep a positive frame of mind, because God will work with that. Look not just at your body, but also at your soul, which is eternally youthful. Dwell there.

***Q: How can we be more aware of our connection to the creator and share more fully with others the love out of which we were created?***

SG: To find God, who is invisible silent energy, you have to become very quiet and still. God cannot be perceived in the outer world except indirectly through the creation. To know God personally, you must meet God inside of yourself—heart to heart and love to love. If you buy all the flowers in the world and see how beautiful they are, you may conclude that God is beautiful, but that is not the same as meeting God face to face. Jesus met God face to face in the temple of himself, and he fervently wanted the people of his time to understand how to become living temples of God. You are living temples of God, so stop looking outside of yourself to find happiness, to find peace, or to find God.

Meditate, meditate, *meditate*. This will take you inside and higher and higher into the superconscious mind where you will find your own God presence. You will be bathed in the love of God that fills and surrounds you. You will be impregnated with this love so that you can give it to others. Love others as yourself. Empathize by putting yourself in the other person's place. Sometimes we in spirit think that the answers are so simple that they elude intelligent ones on earth who think life must be more complex.

Though some are singled out by us for certain spiritual work, you are all born with spiritual gifts, and you all need to awaken to your spiritual senses in order to awaken to your true self. When you meet people, feel that they are you. Become them. From your solar plexus, feel their presence and energy. You will receive the message of who they are and it will be registered and deciphered through your third eye. Some of you know this already. If you have a gut feeling, it means you have received a message, but you don't always recognize it as such or use it in a metaphysical way for your betterment.

Jesus felt beyond measure the pain of others and could look deeply into their souls because he looked deeply into his own soul. He took on such great suffering that for all time and eternity he could empathize with people and know their pain. If you love others as yourself, you can't help but be touched by their suffering. You will step in to help, not out of moral obligation, but because you feel their pain.

***Q: How can we learn to surrender completely to God?***

SG: Where is your hunger? In your stomach? In your heart? In your mind? One way to surrender deeply is to spend time in spiritual service. When Mother Teresa was asked how she could do her work, she said that she just looked into the eyes of suffering individuals, and she could see Christ. Often, individuals do not completely surrender until they have suffered. They pay a karmic price that helps us usher them to the place of surrender.

When you finally awaken to the fullness of who and what you are, there will come a time when you will feel broken. Sometimes this happens in stages, and sometimes in one moment. It happens both through your efforts and by the intercessory power of God. When the time is right, all things come together, including the moment of surrender. All the great teachers and saints that I have spoken to and observed in the spiritual world and on earth finally came into their own when they surrendered. They detached from their own desires and let God have his way. They became obedient. What they have in common is the realization that there is *one* will, not two. They surrendered to that one will and found peace. They found miracles. They found perfection.

Philip has been tested by various electronic means and he has been found to stay in a meditative or alpha state much of the time. This is not because he was born this way, but because he has been earnest since childhood about being with God. He has gone into meditation again and again to explore the inner world, asking, "Who am I? Where are you, God?" Through this practice, he has experienced a liberation that is not just theoretical, but based on a genuine breakthrough from theory to fact and from an ideal of God to the reality of God. Through such experiences, we know that God lives within.

When that happens, many cry for hours and days because that which they longed for was present all the time while they were searching for it. I cried endlessly when it happened to me because that which I sought was already mine, yet I had not known it. It is like a man who longs for and misses his beloved, standing beside her with closed eyes, not knowing she is there. When he opens his eyes and sees her, she is no longer an idea in his mind, and he falls upon her shoulder and embraces her with many tears and with so much love, because he has come home. He has found the love of his life.

This is who and what God is: The love of your life. Many want to make God into infinite abstract energy, or intellectual power—something outside and beyond human experience. Not true. Not true. God is all of that and more, but at the core, God is your beloved. King David, with all of his problems, sang praises to God in psalms because in the best times of his life he came into ecstasy with God as a presence within. At those moments, he could converse freely and intimately with God.

If you want to change the world, you must change yourself. A drop of water falling into the ocean will ripple forever. When you drop into the heart and mind of God within yourself and truly experience that marriage, the ripple effect within you and within the universe will be endless. Can you feel this?

Spiritual masters want to teach who God is and where God is, and they will all tell you the same thing. While on earth they may be responsible for specific teachings, but there comes a time when there is a shift due to their continued upward climb. They come face to face with God within, and then all of life changes. Some of the most advanced masters are those from India who taught this principle for eons of time. Once anyone meets God in the way that I have described, nothing else matters, and love with God becomes the center of reality, no matter what happens in the outer plane of life.

The more you turn within and surrender your life to that higher reality, the freer you will be from temptations to do otherwise. Drink from the fountain of spiritual life and raise your consciousness higher. If you do not yet know the infinite power and the unstoppable divine love that courses through you, it is only because you have not reached the highest levels of self-knowledge, as did Jesus, Buddha, and others.

# The Law of Attraction

*Q: Many are teaching and writing about the law of attraction. Is it beneficial for me to visualize my life the way I would like it to be?*

SG: Develop the habit of thinking in terms of affirmations, because the energy that you put out is indeed the energy you get back. That *is* the law. If you fear something, even without intention, it is more likely to come upon you. Conversely, if you maintain a positive outlook and send out positive energy, you will receive that kind of energy in return.

You are always visualizing or imagining, and from our side we see that you imagine negatively much of the time, even unconsciously. Your thoughts, or even your general attitude, may include, "I can't," "This won't happen," "I may fail," "I could have an accident," or "I won't have enough money." Your worrying will not prevent something negative from happening, and it will make you unhappy in the meantime.

When you are down in the dumps, you have a hard time lifting yourself up, though you may try various ways to do so. Chocolate, coffee, soft drinks, cookies and all those things that you love to eat with mayonnaise, ketchup, and bread won't help! What *will* help is to pick up the phone, call someone and ask how he or she is doing. That person will tell you! You know that. Then you are projecting your energy outward. If you try this, you will find that it works. By law—think about it—*by law*, the energy you send out must come back to you. As you seek to lift someone else up, you will be lifted.

Within each of you is something like a truth box that receives the words that I speak, but there is something higher than that—the heart, through which you can feel love coming through to you. Regardless of the content of my message, your heart will be touched because I love you. We are drawn together by the compelling energy of love. This is also part of the reality of the law of attraction.

***Q: Another popular idea is that we create our own reality. Can you explain why some people work very hard at trying to create goodness in their lives without success?***

SG: If people feel a need to create goodness as their reality, they will seek to create it, but life will teach us what we need to learn, and each person's situation is different. Everything that appears on your path is there to teach you about you. If you are robbed of the opportunity to pay off karmic debts or to do your dharma—that which by your nature you feel called to do to be spiritually fulfilled— you will not grow as you were intended to grow in this lifetime. There are certain object lessons that you have to go through in order to get what you came to get. At the deepest level, your will and God's will are one, but you are prevented from completely knowing that one will because you came to earth to grow.

On this kind of question, go within. If you go deep inside, over time you will find the answer to this question, but the answer is not the same for everyone. There are as many paths up the mountain as there are people, and each person has his or her own things to work out. Stay on *your* path, stay centered on working within yourself, and learn to hear the voice within. Do these things until you are sure you are hearing the voice of God within, and you will never be misled. All the masters learned to discern that reality.

The voice I speak of is not hidden; it is clear. You must go deep enough within yourself to hear it. Once you know the presence of God, ask questions, receive answers, and carry on conversations. You may have already done this, but you still don't have a clear picture of the reality of it. If I could lift from your eyes the scales that blind you from seeing this reality, I would. If I did, you would be shocked to realize how real God is, and how much of what you think is real is not, including your fears and perceived inadequacies. You are mighty! You came from the source of all life. You are fundamentally a part of that energy, and it flows through you at all times. It is the sustenance of your being, it is always there, and you cannot live without it. God and humanity are one, and there is no separation. There is only your lack of knowledge, experience, and awareness.

***Q: Is it possible to make mistakes, or is everything truly in the hands of God?***

SG: Even if you make mistakes, you are still in the hands of God. I'll use an illustration I have used before: All children fall down. If that never happened, how would their muscles grow strong enough for them to stand and stay up? Everything you go through happens so that you can learn.

Most people think of life events just as things that happen to them. People who are wise and discerning grow the fastest by learning from the smallest occurrences in their lives. That is why you have to watch and remain alert.

The little things that look like coincidences are often pivotal points for change. Think about it. You learn from the little things that together make up big things. The door of life swings on small hinges, and those little hinges carry the weight of the heavy door. Be observant.

# Meditation and Prayer

***Q: You have said that meditation is very important for our spiritual growth. How should we meditate?***

SG: Various gurus and teachers say that their way is *the* way, but that is not the case. Your own teachers and spiritual masters from the world of spirit are working to usher you toward the method that works best for you. As I have said, most important is consistency toward purpose, obedience, and surrender.

If you are watching a program you like on television, it can be very difficult to pull yourself away, especially if, after a long day at work, you are sitting down to rest. However, those who learn to break through spiritually pray and meditate consistently, even if this means that they must step away from what the majority of people are doing. In this noisy world, who can concentrate? Who can truly get into that finer vibration of spirit, in view of all the distractions of daily life? Mysticism is cultivated away from the world. It is not easy, but you can do it if you are serious about your spiritual life.

To start your spiritual practice, focus on your breathing even for five minutes each day, and then ten minutes or more. In this way, you will quickly learn how to meditate. Gurus all over the world have given many mantras, and you can use any of these or repeat words such as "so calm," saying "so" as you breathe in and "calm" as you breathe out. The important thing is to bring the right and left hemispheres of the brain into complete synchronicity. We know that words ending in either the "m" or "n" sound help bring about such unity within the brain. This is one of the reasons why the word "Om" has such a high reaching spiritual value.

My advice to you is to ask, "Which method of meditation is best for me?" and you will receive the answer. By looking through books and talking to different people you will find your way. Fundamentally, all meditation is the same, but there are different approaches to the practice. Though not all teach this, you will do well to learn to turn your eyes up toward the third eye. For this purpose, you can think of the third eye as being in the center of the forehead or between the brows. Clairvoyance, seeing us and seeing the spiritual world, must come about by the stimulation of the third eye. By practicing meditation regularly, you will find that there is a shift in your consciousness to a higher level, from your conscious to your superconscious mind.

Some seek to break through by drilling many wells all over the place, but you get to the water faster by staying in one place and drilling deeper and deeper. Focus on your effort to break through, concentrate on it, and bring it to fruition.

Demand, if you will, the answers that are waiting for you through your consistent effort. Scripture says that those who worship God must worship in spirit and truth. Instead of being caught up in a set of specific ideas, become spiritually alive. If you are going to reach the ultimate goal of your life, which is God-realization and self-realization, then you will consistently need to apply yourself.

Practically speaking, what I am saying is not complicated. The complicated part is overcoming the inertia within yourself, the disbelief that you can do it. You must have faith that you *can* do it. Whether or not you develop your sensitivity and receptivity enough to break through to the superconscious mind is determined by how much you truly discover and understand yourself by applying these principles.

*Q: What is the proper way to pray?*

SG: True prayer does not require ritual. If you are speaking to someone you love, you don't need images or burning candles, and you don't have to be in a special posture or in particular clothing. Some of these things may enhance your experience emotionally, psychologically, or spiritually, but they are not necessary. When you truly want to connect with someone, what do you do? You speak the truth from your heart. You tell it like it is. God deals in truth and we deal in truth, so never whitewash your situation in prayer. Quietly sit down, kneel, or move into whatever posture you choose, and speak your truth. Let it come from your heart.

Not one drop of prayer goes unnoticed, though not all prayers are answered as we expect, partly because some pray amiss. What God wants to give you is usually far greater than what you are praying for, but to receive that greater thing there is a price to pay. True prayer requires persistence and patience. I say again, speak your truth to a greater awareness, a greater love than your own. Realize that a greater love than our individual love brought everything into existence. Speak your truth to God, however you think of God.

Why do the scriptures say to pray without ceasing? True prayer is the heart's longing for divine love and divine truth. This longing is a seed planted deep in the soul of each man and woman. In true prayer, you will have spiritual experiences with God. When Jesus was in the Garden of Gethsemane, and cried out, "Father, Father, let this cup pass from me; nevertheless, not as I will, but as thou dost will," he was expressing his true life experience of knowing God and communing with God. To Jesus, God was not an ideal or concept, but a real living energy—a real personality with whom and from whom he felt divine love. The experience of that love in prayer is what often compelled him to continue with his mission. Once you have that genuine contact, you can never turn from your direction, and your vibration will be raised to higher and higher levels.

***Q: Can you tell us more about the effects of prayer?***

SG: Prayer is the sending forth of mind and heart energy. To the degree that these energies are propelled by your will to love and care, they cannot help but reach the object of your prayer. If, however, you give only lip service to your prayer, the energy does not go far. When you enter into prayer, put yourself in the place of the individual you are praying for. If there is suffering, move into that energy and feel the pain of the one for whom you are praying. Whatever the need, put yourself in the place of that person, and you will be deeply motivated so that your will, desire, and heart energy will carry your prayer forth. Your prayer energy will reach the target of your prayer, and it will help.

Keep praying. Even the smallest prayer is adding to the reservoir of positive energy throughout the universe. Every little drop counts. If a billion people worldwide prayed sincerely and regularly, the reservoir would be overrunning, and the world would change overnight.

*Q: Do our prayers make a greater difference when we pray in a group than when we pray alone?*

SG: Yes, there is a greater impact when you pray together, but only if there is love. Whether you are praying alone or with a group, you must put your heart into it and empathize with the person or people for whom you are praying.

# *Life in the Spirit World*

***Q: What is the best way to prepare ourselves to move from the earth plane to the spirit world?***

SG: Live before you die—really live! So many are standing in the shadow of other people, worried about what others think and say. Get over it! People are too busy thinking about their own lives to be worried about yours. If you find that some people do gossip about you, they are not true friends anyway. Do the things you want to do, without apology or embarrassment. If you want to take up dancing, dance. If you want to paint, paint. Don't wait until you are on your deathbed and say, "Oh, why didn't I do this or that?" Then it will be too late. Yes, you can do some of these things in the spirit world after you die, but don't wait to do the things that can have eternal value for your soul.

Why are you here on earth if not to have fun as well as to learn? Some people think that if they enjoy life too much, God will go away from them, but this is not true. I am not saying to get involved with unseemly things, but to enjoy the company of others, eat good food, go to a good quality movie, buy that shirt that you like so much, or take a vacation. Just be sure that you do everything in accordance with your priorities, and put your highest priorities first. Lead an orderly life. When you do that, you attune yourself to God, the being of greatest order. You will automatically be led to a greater spiritual awakening, to the things that you are to realize while you are on earth.

***Q: What happens to people when they first pass over? Where do they go?***

SG: It depends on the individual. The spirit world has levels that include all degrees of love and truth. The degree to which you have lived the highest truth absolutely and loved unconditionally is the degree to which you will approach the highest level. The highest truth is to find God within, and you *will* find God within. The highest love is to love God with all your heart, mind and soul. If you pursue the highest truth and love, you will meet God. Those who live this way reach the highest levels on earth and enter the spirit world at these levels. Those who live in complete self-centeredness are in lower realms, and there are all degrees in between.

If you want to know who you are and where you would go if you died at this moment, ask yourself, "How much do I love God? How much do I know God within me?" If you can answer those questions, you will know where you are and how much work remains for you to do before you pass into the spirit world.

This is a serious question, and I do not give this answer with accusation or judgment. It may be sobering to realize what the answer is, but I do not mean for you to eliminate fun and joy from your life. Just balance your life with enough investment in your spiritual learning and growth to guarantee your arrival at the highest possible level within the spiritual world.

***Q: Does each person experience a life review upon arriving in the spirit world? Is it possible to have a life review while still on earth and make amends for wrongs before going to the spirit world?***

SG: Each one of you will ultimately stand before your own consciousness and look into your own soul. Many people fear going into the spirit world because they don't want to face themselves. The best thing to do is to face yourself during this life. Therapy, confession, talking things through, journaling about your life and being honest with yourself can help you to expiate things inside that are bothering you because they go against what you know to be true, good and loving. It is true that you will face in the spirit world whatever problems you do not work through while you are on earth.

You must realize this: There is only *now.* All the former nows are gone except *this* now, and the only thing that remains from your past is your memory of it. Do you have some responsibility for it? Yes, there is karma, but you *cannot* go back and change the past. Therefore, whenever possible, do good things *now.* Your twelve-step programs say that you should make amends to those whom you have hurt, and it is good to do that where possible. However, if you have cut someone off in traffic out of anger and driven away, you can't tell the person that you're sorry. In that case, God sees the intent in your heart. You may ultimately meet the other driver in the spirit world, and if you are truly sorry in your heart of hearts, the person will know that. The energy you have sent forth will reach that soul without fail.

Also, stop doing things that are wrong. Just stop it, as much as you can. Build from this day forward a life free of things that you know are against the law of self and God—things that create negative karma for you. Is it easy? No. But that is why you are on earth. You are here to master the lower self. Ultimately, you will experience your higher self, which is all light, which knows no mistakes, and which has perfect insight. When you see people who have reached this point, people in whom God's presence is apparent, you see more of God in them than they are often able to see in themselves.

You will learn that from wrong understanding comes wrong thinking and wrong action, which brings negativity, evil and destruction on earth. There are times when you say to yourself, "Why did I do that? I knew better!" or, "Why didn't I just bite my tongue?" It happens all the time. Better to have a bloody tongue than to speak in a way that hurts someone. If you stop yourself and really look at your thoughts, then you can eliminate words and actions that will cause you to experience a life review that makes you regret how you used your life energy.

***Q: Will we see our loved ones when we arrive in the spirit world? Do families live together there?***

SG: Those who are together find love in common at the same level and to the same degree. You already experience this on earth. Sometimes you feel closer to a friend than you do to someone in your own family. Isn't that true? What does that tell you? In the spirit world, you are drawn to people with whom you have associated in life and people with whom you have exchanged your heart. You will be with those whom you have loved the most and those who have loved you the most. This is not a matter of decision, but the application of a principle or law, just as gravity is a law. You cannot break the law of gravity and you cannot break the law of love. Love is the guiding principle that determines attraction.

The ruling principle in the spirit world is the same as on earth, though in spirit it is more exacting and applies to everything without fail. On earth, people can hide behind a mask of pretense simply because they don't want to be honest, don't want to hurt someone's feelings, or any number of reasons. Deception motivated by kindness may be all right, but some people hide their true thoughts or feelings about others for negative reasons.

As I have said, there are many realms in the spirit world. The inhabitants of a particular realm have an essential nature reflected by that realm. Each person's degree, level, and kind of love will determine who is drawn to each realm. Those most closely drawn together will be those who most intensely loved each other. There can be spiritual or physical attraction, as it is with husband and wife, but in any case, you will find yourself with people who are at the same level of love as you.

***Q: If we love someone who died without the degree of love you described, will we be able to find that person when we pass into the spirit world?***

SG: Absolutely. Wherever anyone is in the spirit world, two people can meet if the one in the higher realm goes to the lower realm, but not the other way around. Beings in lower realms cannot go to higher realms until they have advanced spiritually to that level. Those in the twelfth grade can go down to lower grades of learning with ease, but someone who is in the second or third grade cannot go into a twelfth grade class and learn. The second or third grader has to gain the merit of passing grades, one by one, to go to the highest level, the twelfth grade.

***Q: What is life like in the spirit world? Is clothing worn? What do we do there?***

SG: What people do with their life energies while on earth determines where they go and what it is like for them in the spirit world. Those who have committed crimes against others or themselves and those who have generated negativity by being selfish and judgmental will be in a lower realm, reflecting how they have thought and lived on earth. In the lower realms of the spirit world, there are all shades of darkness, from a greater to lesser degree. A person who steals from his neighbor is likely to be in a darker realm than he would have been if he had not done that, and he may be overshadowed by an awareness of his act. If someone has killed another out of selfishness, that person will be in a still darker state, very different from that of the spirit of someone who has lived a life of goodness.

You will have an idea of the highest levels of the spirit world if you think of sunlight that is brilliant and yet doesn't hurt your eyes. From the highest realms, where all is light, imagine coming down to the realms of light in which it is only as bright as your earthly daytime. There is every shade or degree of light and they all represent levels of love and truth.

You will see topography, flowers, fruit, animals, houses, clothing, furniture, boats and most other things that exist for people on earth. These realities become more beautiful and rarified as you go up the scale of love and truth to the higher realms. In the highest realms, you experience limitless light and limitless love, where everything is seen and known to be from one source.

In the highest realms, there is a state of great contemplation where everything fades, including self in its finite form. Self is experienced as infinite being with no barriers and no limitations. Self becomes a being of love, having access to the highest truth and to all wisdom. Self can then look upon humanity with the eyes and heart of a parent, with great compassion and great love. In the presence of such beings, a constant vibration of love and prayer issues forth. Thoughts and blessings emanate from them, broadcasting out to all of humanity on earth and in the spirit world.

Our spiritual clothing reflects the level of love and truth of each realm. The material and brightness of color used in clothing worn by those in the highest levels is made of pure light. Everything is light in the spirit world. In the lesser realms, the light is dimmer and of a coarser nature, and in the higher realms, it is the purest and brightest light. If you have a vision of someone like Archangel Michael, Jesus, Buddha or any being of such a nature, you see abundant light of beautiful colors. This reflects the condition of the hearts and minds of those spiritual beings based on what they have done with their lives. The same principles apply throughout all the realms of spirit.

The spirit world is as unlimited as your thoughts. It is a place where thoughts register and solidify to create heaven, hell, and everywhere in between.

***Q: What happens in the afterlife to someone who commits suicide?***

SG: Though it might surprise some of you to hear it, each situation is different. What would you think about someone who is lying in bed, suffering night and day? On earth, particularly in America, such people are not allowed to take enough of certain medicines to eliminate the pain, even when they are in so much pain that they can think of nothing else. They cannot take another moment, because they are in such torture. Should they live it out? Continue to suffer? It is up to them, of course.

I am not saying that it is correct to take your own life,

but you asked about the consequences of doing that. If you were God and you were watching, how would you judge a person who committed suicide because of extreme, unremitting pain? Would you judge such a person severely, or with deep care and concern? With understanding? With condemnation? With *compassion*—greatest compassion!

What if a man receives bills in the mail that come to a total greater than the amount of money he has in the bank, and he has no way to pay his debt? He is so afraid that his neighbors, friends, relatives, and others will find out that he shoots himself or takes a bottle of pills. What about such a person? You may not agree that his situation justifies such an act, but you do not really know why he did it. Out of ignorance? Fear? What is the reason? How would you judge him? How should you look upon him? With compassion!

Intent is always a part of evaluating what a person does, and intent can really be known only by God. The man who steals a loaf of bread because he is lazy is different from the man who steals it because he has no money and his family is starving. Would you judge the two the same? As you can see, it is case by case, and only God knows each human heart.

Do not interpret my words to mean that suicide is the thing to do. I am talking about how to look at it if it does happen. One should never take one's life if it is possible to go on, even in great suffering, because there is a benefit to you if you can endure and put everything into the hands of God. *That* is the secret.

***Q: Some people have committed acts such as kidnappings, rapes, or molesting children. What happens to them when they die?***

SG: They are already in the hell of their own minds, and they enter a self-created hell in the spirit world. They are isolated behind bars of their own making, their own thinking and their own feeling. Ultimately, all will experience a life review where they can empathize with their victims and feel the full extent of the suffering they have caused. This will result in self-judgment, self-imprisonment, and the beginning of their ability to change. Wherever they are in this process when they die, they will go to a realm in the spirit world that exactly reflects their level of spiritual growth and the life they have lived. This is true for all of humanity.

Even in cases like this, it is possible to feel compassion. Such people are still children of God, and only God knows the cause of the aberration within them. Was the individual molested or abused as a child? Were there physical or mental imperfections that attracted darker spirit beings who intensified their inclinations? Such spirits may have shoved, pushed, pulled, and compelled the person to act out. From our side we see that happening frequently.

In the lower realms of spirit, there are darker souls who engaged in demonic behavior when they were on earth. They enjoyed the suffering of others and committed acts that caused suffering. People on earth who have been punitive toward self and others lower their own vibrations to the extent that such spirits can invade them. They open their own electrical energy field, their auras, to spirits from the lower realms who have similar vibrations. Such spirit beings can influence them to act in ways that feed into their own inclinations.

Your prisons are filled with individuals who are tortured by their deeds but cannot overcome because they are so obsessed and possessed by lower entities. Many who are executed or who die in prisons leave their bodies with no way to expiate their anger, sorrow, and pain. By the energy that they retain, they are drawn back to the prison to cause more agitation and destruction, thereby generating more negative energy. In this way, it becomes a vicious cycle.

We are busy going to the lower levels of the spirit world trying to shine upon the minds of individuals there with information and love. We do whatever we can to get a spark of light into their hearts so that they might look up and look out. Most of them are turned inward to such a degree, with so much self-hate, that it may take eons of time for them to change, unless we can help them to come out of this state.

We have pity on individuals who hurt themselves and others. This does not mean they should not be punished, but the punishment used in your prison system on earth is based on a lack of understanding of how people change. Such individuals should be restrained so that they cannot cause further harm, but they should also be educated, enlightened, and placed in a quiet atmosphere where they can begin to be aware of their true situation. In prisons on earth, I have observed shouting, crying at night, wailing, pounding on bars, all kinds of profanity and more. How can anybody be rehabilitated under such circumstances?

I could say much more about all of this. For now, I will say that I lean toward compassion for these individuals because I have seen how they were victims themselves. I am maintaining my composure now, but I have often wept over people who are prisoners of their own minds, and that includes all of us at times. They *do* have to pay. It is the law of karma, the law of love; but you know what is said, "Every saint has a past, and every sinner has a future."

# Spirit Guides and Teachers

***Q: Can you tell us more about spirit guides, including the guides that work with Philip?***

SG: I would advise you to include the reality of spirit guides and teachers in your understanding of life. Spirits are able to pass on their thoughts and feelings to people on earth, and you can't always distinguish between what is coming from them and coming from your own mind. This is especially true if you have no awareness of their existence or their way of relating to you. Are you aware of the air going in and out through your nose unless you focus your mind on your breathing? Our overshadowing of many of you is so subtle that it may go unnoticed unless you have developed fine attunement to the spirit world.

When the auric field is open, lower entities can come in and cause a person to be misinformed, confused, afraid, and even obsessed or possessed, so it is always good to pray and ask for spiritual protection. If you do this when you meditate, we can come to intercede on your behalf.

As for the four spirit guides who work with Philip, we are less concerned about our identity than about truly representing the pure, unselfish love of God, but since you asked, I will tell you about us. Black Hawk is a Native American guide whose mission is to guard and protect Philip spiritually. He moves around or stands nearby when Philip is in a trance or semi-trance state, protecting him from lower entities that might otherwise come into his energy field.

Kathryn Kuhlman, another of Philip's guides, was one of the greatest spiritual healers who ever lived. She came to Philip in a dream and said, "I will do everything here in the spirit world that I can, giving my whole life to help you succeed in your mission." She comes all in white and stands to his right at all times when he is doing this work.

Dr. Daniel David Palmer, the founder of chiropractic, is one of Philip's guides. In his own literature, he says that he received the chiropractic method from the spiritual world, and that is true. When Philip is doing readings on the telephone, Dr. Palmer will go out from Philip, bringing a green light to heal individuals in distance. Philip clairvoyantly sees that happening.

I am also Philip's guide, and the four of us work as a team. Others come, and an outer band of teachers and guides works with him. In the beginning, Philip was surprised when several mediums gave him spiritual messages that included names of individuals in the spirit world who were working with him. These mediums were quite accurate, and it would take five to ten minutes for them to name all the spirits that came. The wider your mission, the greater the number of spirit individuals who will be working with you.

If you get a reading from someone who is able to tell you about your spirit guides and teachers, then your awareness of them and your ability to communicate with them will increase. This could be important in your life from our point of view, but you can decide this for yourself.

***Q: How are you able to speak directly to us through another human being?***

SG: People use intelligence to register and calibrate all information through their atomic, molecular structures. We in the spirit world are also made of atoms and molecules, as well as elements that you do not have on earth. We are therefore able to interpenetrate the physical world by coming into the configuration of atoms and molecules that make up your vibration.

With the help of teachers in the spirit world and through my own adeptness, I lower my vibration to come into Philip. He has worked with me in this way so often that there is no disruption for him and he stays in a peaceful state. Because of his experience and his essential nature, I can slip into him as easily as a hand slips into a glove.

Philip has raised his frequency for this experience. He is often at this level because he has heard and perceived the spirit world in multiple ways from childhood to the present. Because he is easily able to come to this level, we can meet each other half way. I am in synchronization with his vibration and he with mine. I am impregnated into his thoughts, feelings, and vocal cords. Spiritual doctors, teachers, and chemists surround him to protect his overall physicality, including his heart and lungs, and to make sure there is enough moisture in his mouth as I speak. There is more I could say, but in simple terms, that is how it is done.

Some people think of this experience as good acting or as a mind game, but that is not the case. Many mediums have clairvoyantly seen me overshadow Philip, watching him leave his body and watching me come into it.

***Q: Can a spiritual master speak directly through anyone as you are doing now?***

SG: Because of the nature of human beings the answer is theoretically yes, though your spiritual and physical DNA makes some of you more or less sensitive and capable of being a channel through whom we can speak directly. Could you be a virtuoso on the piano? Yes or no, depending in part upon your innate talent, but also the extent to which you practice. In the same way, to varying degrees, you can all be channels.

Through the chakra system, which exists within all human beings, your spirit interpenetrates your body. Your spirit is also connected to your physical body by a line of energy that clairvoyants call "the silver cord." When you focus on spiritual things such as God, goodness, love, and service, you bring yourself to the highest levels of the chakra system where full illumination is possible. As I said, each person is already overshadowed by spirit. We come to you from a high level of the spirit world to impress, inspire, and encourage you. The word "inspiration" originates from the words "in spiritus," meaning "in spirit."

Even as much as I am here overshadowing this gentleman, so you too are overshadowed by your spiritual teachers. You may not be equipped to allow a spirit to take over your being and speak through you, but you are animated by spirit, your own guides and teachers, through your thoughts. You are often moved by inspiration from us as we whisper into your spiritual ears. You are moved in your heart. Rely upon that.

# Relationships

***Q: How can we work with others to help raise their level of consciousness if they are not interested in meditating?***

SG: It is not your job to raise the level of consciousness of other people. Each person is responsible to take in information, recognize it as truth, accept it, and apply it in life. Though this may sound paradoxical, to love others, you must love yourself first. You need to take care of yourself and continue to awaken to your own consciousness—your own higher self.

Even though we talk about the spirit world and the physical world as separate things, they are one world. There is one energy. Tune into that energy, the highest of highest energies, as you go through the vicissitudes of life that are necessary to remove layers of falsehood. When you take care of yourself first and raise yourself up in that way, you will acquire the sensitivity and awareness that will help you to know how best to serve others. You will know what to say. When Jesus sent his disciples out, they asked, "What shall we say?" He said, "You will be given what to say."

***Q: How can we respond to those with whom we have a difficult relationship?***

SG: When you experience difficulties or complications in your relationships with others, you sometimes think there is a quick way to change things, but those difficulties may be on your path for a reason. Because all people are different, it is inevitable that you will have disagreements and even conflicts with others, but take them in stride. Rather than to blame the other person, ask what this conflict reflects in you that you can work on.

Above all, keep your ego out of it. The less that you have a fixed idea about how things should happen, the more things will happen in surprising and good ways. I do not mean that you should be irresponsible or indifferent. Sainthood consists of learning exactly how to walk the fine line between being assertive and being passive, and that ability comes to us as we humble ourselves to the great reality that we are temples of the living God.

In any relationship, do not be judgmental toward those who do not agree with you. Listen. That's what I do. When people come to this medium for readings, I listen, sometimes for a long time, before I speak to them through Philip. When you meet another, consciously let the energy of unconditional love flow directly from your heart to the other person. Do that the next time you meet someone and watch what happens. God is in others as much as he is in you.

I may say some things that seem paradoxical, but that is also the path of the masters. Great gurus whose personalities appeared to be defective have raised students and disciples who have done great work. Do not be fooled by outer appearances or become caught up in personality, but stay focused on the truth. You may applaud me because I have been on the path longer, but God is no more in me than in you. God did not divide himself so that he put a pinch in some people and a gallon in others. He is in you now, as much as he ever will be, but you are not aware of that reality because of the lack of life experience and knowing how to open up.

*Q: How can we work in harmony as part of a group?*

SG: Do not judge those who do not seem to fit in with a group in the way you would like them to. Be great souls. Be like parents who embrace all their children, regardless of their character, their strengths, or their weaknesses. Just reach out and let people know that you love them. Love is the key. True love means to love others as self, to not see their faults and to love them as they are. It is the sign of a great master, and the secret to working effectively with groups in spite of differences. Enlarge your souls; enlarge your hearts. Remember the saying, "There but for the grace of God, go I."

We in the spirit world know that in the early Christian communities founded by St. Paul and his followers, people sat in a circle to seek contact with spirit. Why would they do that? Because Jesus was in the spirit world. They created this circle of love to gain oneness with each other and to make direct contact with Jesus. They wanted to receive direct answers, unlike what is experienced in most churches or groups today. Paul wrote about their infighting, disagreements, and mistakes, but he also wrote about gifts of the spirit. Which gift did he say was the greatest? Love. Love will solve all problems, and love is the balm that will heal all things. However, true love must also be patient and kind.

Focus on the greater realities. Whether you serve others on a large or small scale, serve the world with *personal* love. Why didn't I say *universal* love? People have said this is the nature of God's love, and energetically speaking, they are correct; but, on another level, there is no such thing. God's love descends into the earth plane to each person, one by one. It comes to each individual in a unique way, touching the heart and changing that person's reality forever.

***Q: How does this advice apply to the relationship of husband and wife?***

SG: Couples come together for different reasons, depending on their level of spirituality, but everyone is attracted by the magnetic power of love. Some people are initially attracted physically, but if they unite in love, that love will be raised up to the heart chakra where it will become spiritual love.

A husband and wife who *never* experience problems in their relationship probably will not have a long marriage because there is no depth in the relationship. It is through struggle that you truly find each other's soul, and without a marriage of the soul, there is no true marriage in God's sight or ultimately in your own.

Marriage starts out often centered in the lower chakras because the center of sexual attraction is in that area. There may be spiritual attraction for highly advanced souls, but usually it starts out as sexual attraction or attraction to personality or facial features. A couple may have a good sexual relationship without having a good spiritual relationship in marriage, but if that couple does not grow spiritually, by whatever means, the energy will not be raised to the higher chakras, and there will not be a marriage of the heart. As they grow older, there must be a marriage of the soul, which is also a marriage of the mind and heart. Unless that happens, the marriage will not be an eternal one.

***Q: While leaders need to be strong, egos can interfere with maintaining good relationships in a group. How does one balance a strong ego with spiritual surrender and humility?***

SG: Life teaches us. If you hurt too many people too often because of ego, life backfires. Soon, not too many people call you on the phone or write to you. *Life teaches.* On the other hand, an ice cutter is built differently than other ships. The front of the ship must be thicker, with steel of greater strength. Sometimes, to get things done, one has to be very strong. Jesus is often portrayed as mild-mannered and very approachable, but deep inside he is very strong, able to do what needs to be done, and not timid or shy. Much depends on the intention behind any action, so you cannot judge manifestations from an external point of view.

In my life on earth, I have been very strong with people to the extent that some would say that I was mean, but my intention was good, and the outcome was good. If I had been silent or passive, the people with whom I was strong would not have gotten the message and would not have been able to change. Their suffering would have been prolonged.

It is each person's responsibility, as it occurs to each one in consciousness, to lead one's own life. I would turn your question around and say to you, rather than being concerned about those you come up against, think about yourself. Think about your own motive and intention, because you can't change others. Sometimes strength is necessary, and sometimes a soft, quiet, loving word is needed. That is where wisdom comes in. A master is one who learns how to help, direct, and touch others in the best possible way. It takes much life experience.

My advice is always to love others as you want to be loved, and that means to be willing to forgive bruises, insults, and discourteous acts as you would want to be forgiven. Many a relationship could be saved if people would just stop acting out, of course, but when you are confronted by someone else, ask in your heart of hearts: "What is their intention?" You may even ask the person. In many cases, those who are bold for goodness and strong for righteousness may appear arrogant, but their intention is good.

Take a broad view of humility. Someone who feels directed to do God's will may do it in a manner that appears gruff and rough to get God's point across. That person may be humble before God, but may not seem humble to you. The ideal of humility that we associate with St. Francis takes much life experience and wisdom. My recommendation, which I have followed on more than one occasion, is this: When someone is bothering you, or is very confrontational, you have every right to ask the person, "What is your intention? Is it possible that if you approach this in a way that is less confrontational and more loving and humble, you might more easily get your way, or that we all might hear you better?" Be creative. Be creative!

In the end, it is my long experience that mastery is about mastering self, not others, and that includes loving others as you would want to be loved, whether or not they are humble. Sometimes it takes a broken spirit, such as a tremendous fall, or an intense confrontation, before people realize how they affect others.

# Religion

***Q: What is the role of religion?***

SG: Religion is a means, not an end, whereas on earth it has become an end. What is the proper role of religion? Should it cause us to give a great deal of money, or tithe, and to obey its directives? Some who do those very things can become victims, and so it is around the world.

I am not diminishing the value of true religion in its various forms. To sincerely go before God at the altar and genuflect or burn candles is beautiful. In the Far East, I have watched people do obeisance before a figure whom they love and believe in as a manifestation of God, and that also is beautiful. We see the heart, humility, and desire people have to give up their lives to a higher understanding and a higher existence, and we honor that. On the other hand, rituals for the sake of rituals or sermons that repeat the same things do not cause individuals to grow.

Your spiritual progress happens not by following someone, but by going inside and discovering who you are. We urge you to climb the ladder of self, up the chakra system, higher and higher into your awareness, to your superconscious mind. There you will discover that you have always been a being of light, and that only your ignorance has shut the door to your awareness of this.

Once you have discovered that God is within you and that in fact you are God come to earth in this form, why is religion needed? Why is the church, temple or synagogue needed? Those who reach this level may still participate for social reasons, and that is good if it is pleasing to them or helps them to be of service to others. They have no further need for ritualistic prayers, instruction or guidance in the form of religion because they are in touch with their own God presence, which guides them night and day. You can call that presence the still, small voice, but it is higher even than that.

The individual who is consistently aware of God within knows precisely what to do and when and how to do it, and there are no mistakes. All things will come as needed to the person who has reached that level of awareness, because that person has become love. This state of being fulfills and transcends religious teachings.

***Q: People have fought wars in the name of religion throughout much of human history. Will this ever change?***

SG: Some religions are man-made, not God-made, and have been used for selfish ends. One of my greatest concerns when I was on earth was the freedom of individuals and groups to worship God in their own way so that each could find God in the innermost self. I sought to pioneer the awareness that God is within. I still teach the reality that as you go inside you find the God presence, an energy that is always there. God is the center of your higher self. This is true religion.

Suffering and wars involving religion often have to do with each side believing it is *right.* Religious wars are largely based on how individuals are interpreting Christian, Islamic, Jewish or other religious beliefs. Religion also has a political aspect, and adherents often see their view as the only view. The fact is that God exists in each person as much as in another and in each country as much as in another. Once we are attuned to the inner self, we know this experientially. If everyone truly understood and experienced this, there would be no war. If individuals who have caused war would look deep within themselves and find their own God presence, divine love itself, there is no way that they could lead the world into war, or cause people to be hurt or killed.

When you focus your existence in the outer world, and judge that world by external standards, there is no way that you can find God within. When religions stop placing preachers, priests, or whomever in positions to be followed, and instead place God as the true object of love above all, then and only then will true religion come to earth. Only then will humankind awaken fully to the value of each individual, regardless of religion, race, language, nationality or anything else.

***Q: Some religious teachings emphasize the angry face of God and punishment for sin. How can people from such traditions learn to know the loving God?***

SG: Everyone needs the answer to that question. You fear God as the result of your not knowing the God of compassionate, unending, unconditional love who condemns no one. You would not know this compassionate God if you only study the teachings of many religions that exist on earth. This is another reason that you must go inside, prayer by prayer, and meditation by meditation, literally to find God within. Jesus found God within, and said so. You can too. Jesus found God by going inside and isolating himself from the world in prayer and meditation. You can too.

# The Future

***Q: We have heard predictions of turmoil in the coming years. Can you tell us what is going to happen?***

SG: I hear the question often, and though I care, I come from a place that is above these concerns. The masters are masters because they understand that this life is a projection. When you stay in your own loving, positive frame of mind, you will not be affected by anything negative that happens in the future. Remember the law that you draw to yourself what you are. People can influence their own future by drawing certain realities to themselves according to what they do or do not believe.

Fear *does* draw to you things that will hurt you, whereas faith will draw to you things that will guide and help you. Attitude is not a small part of this venture of life, but figures greatly in what will happen to individuals and to the world collectively. Your newspapers and other news media sometimes generate a fear vibration, causing an insecure feeling to fall over your nation and the world. This is creating actual trauma within the hearts of people and paralyzing many to such an extent that some are ready to either leave the land or just give up. Do not give in to an attitude of fear.

Predictions notwithstanding, the most important thing is to love yourself to such an extent that you will be grounded in self-understanding. With that kind of integration, higher revelation will come to you. Many people understand things they read in books, but they don't have the experience to understand themselves. The highest truth is to know yourself, and this will cause you to live well now. In living one day at a time, you will find that the future exists *only* in the now.

People often ask me for specific predictions about the future, but dear friends, you have to live out your life, regardless of external events. You have to walk your road and pay your karmic debt in order to advance on your spiritual path. Spend time and energy in the present. How will you grow if your focus is always in the future—a place where you can never really be? You may take precautions to be physically and emotionally prepared for any eventualities, but the fact is that you must go through what you must go through and live your life as it happens to you. If you have all the answers ahead of time, how can you be tested? How will you achieve *self*-mastery so that, no matter what happens, you will not be undone?

When Philip channeled me on the radio at the turn of the millennium, people called in during the days prior to New Year's Eve and asked about a shift or other changes they could expect. My answer was that the universe is not ruled by a man-made calendar. This date had meaning to those who gave it meaning. Some were in such remote areas that they were not aware of a change in the calendar year. Now, many are asking similar questions. Life is dependent upon dharma and karma. Instead of asking what the future holds, it is much more important to ask yourself the questions, "Am I doing my dharma? Am I doing things that will cause me to have to pay back karma that I am creating now?" Nothing will happen to anyone that does not reflect that person's spiritual accounting sheet.

Nothing that you go through, even death, can destroy the essential *You*. Your divine self is the only thing that there really is. It is the spark of who you are. This outer garment is the character you have been given and the costume that you wear. As consciousness touches what it creates, it makes the creation seem real. It is similar to when you have a dream so vivid that you wake to look around and see if it is real. Who created that? You created the dream by projecting it out. When you looked at it, it seemed so real that it even caused an emotional stir within you. Dreams teach us, and we learn from them if we are wise. This life teaches us as we live it out. You have to live out the dream, even if it sometimes seems like a nightmare. When you do, you will come into an ocean of light. That is your destination.

I speak to you in direct connection to that ocean of light. If you could see spiritually, you would see an emanation of energy that is not just Saint Germain, but also a God force, a presence of Father/Mother God. Whatever you want to call it, it is divine love. If you are attuned and spiritually open, you will feel this, because I bring it in my wake. It is with me because I am immersed in that love at all times.

With my presence and words, I am affecting the vibration, both consciously and unconsciously. A higher vibration is going through each one of you and lifting you up, challenging you. Everything is vibratory. You may have heard some of these things before, but they bear repeating many times. Keep thinking and acting positively. Do not stop. Believe in your own power and stay centered upon goodness. Love others as yourself.

***Q: Is there anything we can do to be prepared for whatever the future brings?***

SG: Once again, you draw to yourself what you are, so if you have great anticipation, you can draw something to you and make it happen. My advice is to live well this day. Live one day at a time. Stay away from speculation and prophecy about the future, because no one really knows the timing of things. Even mediums often receive only partial knowledge. That is why Philip gives prophetic information only if we show him something in clear, emphatic terms because a person will benefit greatly from it.

Don't spend your time concerned about the future. Change will come to those for whom change is to come. Those who are to lose money will lose it, those who are to gain it will do so, and those who are to have accidents or other challenges will have those experiences. Such occurrences will have nothing to do with a day or year on the calendar. While there are those who will go through difficulties, others will not be touched at all.

My advice to you is to seek God first. You shall be taken care of, whether you live or die. No matter what happens, seek God's counsel, love and presence first. If you do this, your life will reach the highest attainment possible, which is peace. What the world longs for now, more than money, discoveries, outer space exploration, food or anything else, is peace. People want peace, even though many of them are hungry and do not have shelter. Still, if they could find a moment of peace, it could go a long way in helping them to feel a sense of wellbeing. Find peace through finding God and share this peace with others. The peace that you give is the peace that you will get back.

The best way to face the future without fear is to live your life based on a deep and genuine relationship with God. If you are focused on God and center your life on God, what is there to fear? If you are living with God in the present, how can the future harm you?

***Q: Can we human beings affect weather conditions and natural disasters through spiritual practices?***

SG: There are those among you who can cause rain to fall, but everything happens in accordance with spiritual principles and spiritual law. When karmic debt is paid, areas that are intended to get rain will get rain. What happens in the meantime? One governor in a state where there was a drought asked the people to pray for rain. Would that have happened otherwise? No. Through these prayers, what more could happen? Miracles. People who had not been praying could experience spiritual breakthroughs and be lifted up to a new level of being, and when enough people pray wholeheartedly, spirits may come in great numbers to intercede on behalf of those who are praying. Each of you has great power, more than you know, but the unleashing of that power cannot come prematurely.

It has been true in the past and will remain true that it is not necessary for all of humanity to respond to God's direction in order to change the world. It takes a relative few, perhaps several thousand, to shift the spiritual axis of the earth toward a positive outcome. As unlikely as it may sound to you, if enough people generate positive energy, this will result in positive outcomes for them and for humanity. As the author of all life, God is in charge of all life. You are an extension of God on earth, and God's work is your work, so what can you do? Be positive. Do not create earthquakes in your own life, and do not create war within your own self. Do not create bad weather within your own thinking.

I'm not saying there won't be significant shifts in the energy surrounding the earth, but there have already been tsunamis, tornadoes and hurricanes aplenty due to the changes in the environment, and some say due to humankind. Rather than worrying about the shift of things, stay in the now. Pray for humanity. Pray that everyone awakens to the reality of the spiritual reasons as to why things happen. Spiritual truth is as solid as any science: As you sow, so you reap. Keep your focus on your path. I learned this principle through many experiences on the earth plane, and we teach the same principle in the spirit world.

Your prayers provide a vibration that helps us to come in great numbers to intervene in the energy surrounding the earth. Don't focus on the outcomes of your prayers for the earth, just pray without ceasing, and you will see immediate benefits within yourself. Trust that we are present, working constantly behind the scenes with all praying people, to bring healing and uplifting frequencies to Mother Earth, to all of humanity, and to you.

*Q: Will time, as we know it, come to an end?*

SG: The age in which you are living now is the age in which people will realize that there is no such thing as time, and that only the now exists. You have already heard much about that, and various movements that are characteristic of this age will teach about it. There will be a greater awakening within humanity to the importance of living now, as people fully realize that solving life's problems has nothing to do with the past or the future. Memory is about yesterday, and that which happened does not exist anymore. When you carry guilt from yesterday instead of doing what you can to correct it, then you prolong your own suffering. There is only now, and there is no future or past.

If you have not already done so, truly examine the fact that there is only now. As long as you think that there is yesterday, then you drag your past with you. As long as you think there is tomorrow, you will procrastinate about doing the things that you should do now. When you scatter your energies by dwelling in the past, which is just a memory, or fantasizing about the future, you will fail to focus your energies on the here and now, and may fail to do things that you need to do to be successful. Many of you are aware that you do that, so say to yourself, "Do it now. Do it now." I'm not saying to wear yourself out doing everything now. Do one thing at a time.

It is not as though time existed in ages past and it does not exist now. Even in the past only now existed, but there was not the awakening to that reality. Today we have electrical, mathematical, and astronomical sciences, and quantum physics, all of which are helping us to understand that traditional concepts of time are limited. Through science, humanity has become knowledgeable and more aware of how things actually work. God is the greatest scientist. He created everything out of much scientific forethought, combined with divine love.

***Q: Do you think that the world is becoming more spiritually evolved?***

SG: If you only read the newspapers and watch television, you might as well slit your wrists and come here now. However, the bad behavior and bad news are a very small portion of all that is happening. There are not enough newspapers in the universe to publish all the acts of compassion, the reaching out, and the good deeds happening among humanity.

We feel very pressed to get humankind to awaken to what it is doing to itself through the vibrations of what is published and aired on television and radio. To counter this, keep contributing your good energy. Instead of thinking so much about whether or not humanity is evolving, think about your own spiritual evolution and the role you play within the whole. Go inside, look at your motive or intent, and observe yourself objectively.

When you meet people, love them. Just love them. When adversity crosses your path, look at it, swallow it up, and give thanks for it. It is paying off karma in a way that will ultimately benefit you and others.

Love yourself. Be happy that you are you. Watch over yourself as a parent would watch over and correct a child as needed. By doing this you will discover yourself. Each of you is an individual, as I am. You are an individual expression, a radiation of the God presence. Taken all together, you are God. As you follow your light from its origin and back to its source, you will see it is all one light.

# Bringing God to the World

***Q: How can we influence the world for good in this life?***

SG: War, disease, starvation, and unkindness are still among you, but humankind will come to know God in this age. Wherever you go, you can influence the world just by your positive energy. This is why I am here, and it is what I have come to teach. It is the end goal of what we are all about. You can pray for others, and prayer has a very positive effect. Send out good thoughts to people if you are not used to praying formally. If you are used to praying, write down the names of others on a piece of paper and call each name out, asking God to bless each one, each day. Call on us to help and protect others and guide them on their way. It is not complicated.

When you pray, ask that more people will come into the direction of love and higher wisdom, and ask for your own wisdom in helping this to happen. You are not responsible for another person's awakening, but prayer makes a difference. It will change you, and that will in turn influence and change others. I encourage you to stay the course and you cannot fail. I am playing a universal role by working with many individuals and groups. I want people to know that their seeking with a sincere heart is invaluable to God and to the spiritual world. It does make a difference.

Change comes about by what means? Change! People have difficulty because they believe that *thinking* about change will bring it about, but it will not. If you want to be out of a room you are in, you can't get out by thinking about it. You have to get up and walk out. If you want to send out a loving vibration to others and maintain that vibration in your own life, don't interact with the negativity of this world because it will bring you down. Be aware of how you use the precious life you have been given. Do not spend time taking in negative energy in any form, whether it is radio, television, print media, or spending time with negative individuals. Is this wise? Yes. Unless you have a practical need for the negative information that comes from any source, why participate in it and let it assault your spirit?

I am a positive presence in whom there is no negativity. How did I get to this state? I did it by staying on the golden path, which is all light, all love, and all truth. I will not veer from it. To the degree that I can cause anyone else to stay on the golden path of life, I will do so. I am dedicated to helping others do the same thing I have done.

***Q: People long for world peace. Will peace ever come on earth?***

SG: War in the world reflects the war within human beings. Peace on earth is a reflection of the peace inside each person. March for peace if you are moved to do so; but make sure that as much as you march outside, you march inside—straight into your own heart—to establish equilibrium and peace within. Find the balance within yourself through which peace is possible. Peace will never come on the face of the earth until everyone has it inside. You can put all the armaments down and turn all your swords into plowshares, but war will rise up again, as it has throughout history, until human beings go inside and find the God presence within.

Pray first for peace within yourself. There is no question that any and all sincere, correctly motivated prayers for world peace make a difference, first in the people praying and then in the world. Therefore, never fail to pray. Prayer is the heart's expression out into the ethers of the universe. In the final reality, whether or not your prayers bring peace to the world, they will bring peace to you.

# Afterword—Saint Germain

I HOPE THAT MY WORDS have not just enlightened you, but that in some part of your soul, you have been moved to a deeper realization of who you are. I am a master, not because I am superior, but because I was especially called out, and I listened. When I listened, sincerely and deeply, I heard what I needed to hear, and I obeyed. There is actually no other path to success in life but that. It is the means to achieving self-liberation and perfection.

We on this side are grateful that many want to learn from our coming through in this way. If this were to happen around the world, then a great change could come about, but don't worry about that. Be happy that you are moving toward integration and higher understanding. You are becoming free from ignorance and coming closer to true love and to God. Find peace in that.

Please, please come to know God within you, and learn what that means. God is just a word—come to know *love* within you.

Never miss a chance to reach out to another soul, to another person. Never pass someone by that you could help with a kind word or deed. This is the Christ nature. It is not about words and concepts, but about giving out from your soul. It is about loving yourself enough so that you are able to love others as much or more than you love yourself.

When you go to bed tonight and lay your head on your pillow, go deep inside and find the light that is there—that has always been there. Dwell in that profound peace. There you shall find all of heaven.

Thank you for this wonderful opportunity to be with you through this channel. God bless you for your love and diligence in seeking answers. Know always that our love follows you wherever you go.

This is Saint Germain.

# About Philip Burley

Born on Thanksgiving Day, November 23, 1939 in Fort Wayne, Indiana, Philip Burley began having early morning bedside visitations from spirit guides and master teachers at the age of four. In the tradition of many mystics, he felt prompted to pray for others and for the world at this very young age. Philip attributes his spiritual awakening and heightened awareness to his early and ongoing encounters with God and with elevated spiritual beings who have guided him since childhood. His search for God has remained the central focus of his life.

Philip has been a professional medium and trance channeler for more than twenty-one years. He has provided spiritual readings to thousands of individuals and has taught dozens of seminars and lectures on the nature of the spirit world. He is a master teacher of the art of meditation and spiritual development. Best known for channeling spiritual master Saint Germain, Philip has demonstrated the gifts of channeling and mediumship to audiences at educational conferences and on radio shows throughout the United States. He produced and hosted "The Inner View—Adventures in Spirit," one of the top call-in shows in the Phoenix area. It drew an audience from around the world through the radio and the Internet. Philip is the author of the books *To Master Self is to Master Life* and *A Legacy of Love, Volume One: The Return to Mount Shasta and Beyond,* both channeled through Philip by Saint Germain.

Philip lives with his wife Vivien in Phoenix, Arizona and enjoys frequent visits with his three children and seven grandchildren.

# About Saint Germain

Historically, Saint Germain lived in the 1700s during the reigns of King Louis XV and King Louis XVI of France. According to some accounts, he was a close associate of King Louis XV and the son of royalty himself. He took his name from an area in France, so the word "Saint" in his name is unrelated to Christian sainthood. He apparently used several different names, and that has made him an elusive figure in history. He may have traveled incognito as a security measure against thievery or bodily injury, a practice of many wealthy people of his day.

Saint Germain was an accomplished musician, poet, and knowledgeable conversationalist who was keenly interested in political and social issues. He was particularly concerned about human freedom. He believed that everyone has the right to a unique relationship with God, and that no one else should be able to dictate what that relationship should be.

Saint Germain is known as an adept because his contemporaries associated him with extraordinary attributes. He was said to be an alchemist who could change base metal into gold, and more than one noblewoman of his time wrote in her journal that he never seemed to age, appearing to look between forty and fifty years old no matter how much time had passed. Some wrote that he could appear and disappear at will.

In my experience, of course, Saint Germain still *does* appear and disappear at will! On one occasion, he came in a flash of light in my room prior to my channeling him the next day. Though I had been calling out to him, I had not asked him to appear. In the beginning of our relationship, he told me that the time would come when I would not be able to tell where I ended and he began. For me, it is that way now. He is an ever-present, loving, and encouraging mentor, respectfully guiding and coaching me regarding my work and personal life. Over the course of many years, he has won my absolute trust.

When Saint Germain speaks directly through my vocal cords as I give readings, people tell me that his tremendous compassion and deep understanding of their inner experience have a profound healing effect on them. Mediumistic people who observe me channeling him testify to the brilliant purple light and intense energy of love that emanate from his presence.

Whatever the facts are surrounding his historical birth, life, and death, Saint Germain comes today in spirit as a heavenly advisor who consistently represents God's universal wisdom and love for all human beings.

*Mastery Press, Publishers*
*Phoenix, Arizona*

For general inquiries send an email to aim.az.hq@gmail.com, or write to:

Adventures in Mastery, LLC (AIM)
P.O. Box 43548
Phoenix, AZ 85080

To receive information about having a spiritual reading, contact:

readingswithphilipburley@gmail.com

CPSIA information can be obtained at www.ICGtesting.com
Printed in the USA
LVOW061628210312

274166LV00001B/178/P